Table of Contents

Preface

The majority of the human race is both fascinated and intrigued by the concept of angelic and spiritual beings which can both dwell in heaven and travel to this earth. Why is there such a fascination with angels? Where did these heavenly beings originate? What is the role of angelic beings in relationship to mankind? What is their relationship with God, the Father and Jesus Christ? What role do angels play in the lives of men today? The purpose in this series of studies is to give a biblical answer for all such questions relating to angels and other created spiritual beings.

The Word of God clearly reveals the fact that there is a spiritual realm which lies beside and beyond our human realm. It is not necessary to speculate or wonder about angels and demons. The Bible contains solid information about both the bright and dark beings. The intent of this study is to explore everything the Bible says concerning angels and demons, so that our curiosity will be satisfied and our faith will be strengthened.

This study intentionally avoids all human speculation, opinions, and theories concerning angels and their function as God's elect ambassadors. This study attempts to state simply what the Word of God reveals concerning these splendid creatures from God. The author has attempted to give scriptural references for each concept that is presented in this study.

Angels are mentioned in thirty-four different books of the Bible. The word "angel" appears in some form, 305 times in the Bible. The goal of this study is to examine each angel encounter found in God's word and to help the student to come to a greater understanding and appreciation for these divine ambassadors from God.

The author's sincere desire is that this study will bring the student both joy and a greater knowledge and understanding of God eternal plan for mankind, as it has for the author. Angels are wonderful and marvelous creatures whose glory consists in their unique serviceability to the divine will of God.

The author would like to say a special word of thanks for Keith Jones, his brother in the Lord and friend who greatly assisted him in the correction of the final manuscript.

Michael Hardin

Angels

and Other Created Spiritual Beings

by

Michael Hardin

ISBN 10: 1-58427-241-4

ISBN 13: 978-158427241-0

Cover Photo: The cover photo is from a model of the ark of the covenant which had cherubim covering the mercy seat. Photo courtesy of FreeStockPhotos.com.

Guardian of Truth Foundation
P.O. Box 9670
Bowling Green, Kentucky 42101
1-800-428-0121
www.truthbooks.net

The Nature of Angels

The majority of mankind is both fascinated and intrigued by the concept of angels and spiritual beings. Why the current fascination with angels? It's rooted in the fact that we human beings are aware of a spiritual realm which lies beside and beyond our own. It isn't necessary to speculate or wonder about angels and demons. The Bible contains solid information about both the bright and the dark beings. We hope to explore everything the Bible says about angels and demons, so that our curiosity will be satisfied and our faith will be strengthened.

What Is An Angel?

The root word translated "angel," in both the Old and New Testaments, means **_"messenger."_** The Hebrew word, _mal'ak,_ emphasizes the fact that angels are God's agents who represent the One who sends them. Similarly the Greek word, _angelos,_ represents angels as divine messengers, ambassadors sent by God. Faithful angels are obedient servants of God. The importance of both the Hebrew word _mal'ak_ and the Greek word is that both terms describe the function or duty of angels rather than their nature. These words describe an _office_ rather than a nature; they tell us what angels _do_ rather than what they _are._ The Word of God presents angels as a company or host of heavenly beings who are subordinate to God and who share His company and reflect His glory and majesty. "The LORD has established His throne in the heavens; And His sovereignty rules over all. Bless the LORD, you His angels, Mighty in strength, who perform His word, Obeying the voice of His word! Bless the LORD, all you His hosts, You who serve Him, doing His will" (Psa. 103:19-21, NASB).

Angels are the _elect_ ambassadors or emissaries of God. "I solemnly charge you in the presence of God and of Christ Jesus and of His chosen angels, to maintain these principles without bias, doing nothing in a spirit of partiality" (1 Tim. 5:21, NASB).

Angels are presented and discussed only in relation to their function as dutiful servants of the sovereign God. Angels direct our attention to God and not to themselves. The Book of Revelation tells of the Apostle John's attempt to offer worship to an angel. "I fell at his feet to worship him. And he said to me, 'Do not do that!; I am a fellow servant of yours and your brethren who hold the testimony of Jesus; worship God!'" (Rev. 19:10, NASB). Worship is never directed toward an angel in the Word of God. Worship and thanksgiving must always be given to God the Father and Jesus Christ.

Hebrews 1:13-14 tells us that these spiritual beings were created by God

> Worship is never directed toward an angel in the Word of God.

to serve as ministers to us, the heirs of God's salvation. "But to which of the angels has He ever said: "Sit at My right hand, till I make your enemies your footstool"? Are they not all ministering spirits sent forth to minister for those who will inherit salvation?" (Heb. 1:13-14 NKJV). The variety of functions of these spiritual beings can be summarized in their title as found in Hebrews 1:14, i.e. "ministering spirits."

What Is The Function Of Angels?

In general, angels simply do God's bidding, whatever that may be. Angels are not bound by natural laws that limit humans, and they symbolize God's active involvement in the lives of mankind.

What do angels do?

- Angels are helpers and protectors to God's people in need (Psa. 34:7; 91:11).
- Angels come to reassure God's people and to offer hope (Jesus—Matt. 4:11).
- Angels come to give God's people guidance and direction (The Law of Moses—Gal. 3:19).
- Angels come to call men to special missions (Moses—The Burning Bush—Exod. 3:2)
- Angels come to rescue God's people from some great danger (Lot—Gen. 19).

Angels, as intermediaries between God and man, bridge the gap between the unseen world of God and the created world inhabited by man, in order to communicate God's word and will to mankind. "For if the word spoken through angels proved steadfast, and every transgression and disobedience received a just reward, how shall we escape if we neglect so great a salvation, which at the first began to be spoken by the Lord, and was confirmed to us by those who heard Him" (Heb. 2:2-3, NKJV). "The Revelation of Jesus Christ, which God gave Him to show to His bond-servants, the things which must shortly take place; and He sent and communicated it by His angel to His bond-servant John" (Rev. 1:1, NASB).

- Angels have been involved in the world's most important events.
- Angels were involved in the miracles that won Israel's release from slavery in Egypt (Psa. 78:43-51).
- Angels observed the giving of the Law at Mount Sinai (Acts 7:38, 53).
- Angels administered Old Testament Law (Gal. 3:19; Heb. 2:2).
- Angels announced the Savior's birth (Luke 1:5-25).
- Angels ministered to Jesus Christ at Gethsemane the night before His crucifixion (Luke 22:43).
- Angels rolled the stone away from the empty tomb where Jesus had been buried (Matt. 28:1-2).
- Angels announced Christ's resurrection to the women who came to minister to the body of Jesus Christ (Luke 24:1-10).

The function of angels is not limited to earthly activities; they lead all creation in their praise and worship of God. Nowhere is their service to God more perfectly rendered than in their prostration and worship before the divine throne. "All the angels stood around the throne and the elders and

> **Angels were created by God to serve as ministers to us, the heirs of God's salvation.**

the four living creatures, and fell on their faces before the throne and worshiped God, saying: 'Amen! Blessing and glory and wisdom, Thanksgiving and honor and power and might, Be to our God forever and ever. Amen'" (Rev. 7:11-12, NKJV).

The Nature Of Angels

Angels, as inhabitants of the kingdom of heaven, are *spiritual beings,* but they are able to manifest themselves as active and effecting agents in the material world. Angels appear at times as radiant *spiritual beings.* The primary description of angels in Scripture is that of *"spiritual messengers"* or *"servants of fiery flame."* "Who makes His angels spirits, His ministers a flame of fire" *(*Psa. 104:4, NKJV). "But when He again brings the firstborn into the world, He says: "Let all the angels of God worship Him." And of the angels He says: "Who makes His angels spirits And His ministers a flame of fire" (Heb. 1:6-7, NKJV).

When Luke describes the angelic announcement of the birth of the Savior to the shepherds in the field, he speaks of glory and light surrounding the angelic visit. "Now there were in the same country shepherds living out in the fields, keeping watch over their flock by night. And behold, an angel of the Lord stood before them, and the glory of the Lord shone around them, and they were greatly afraid" (Luke 2:8-9, NKJV). The light in which angels make their appearance is not their own raiment, but their clothing from God. The Scriptures attest to angels as visible light and visible glory, although not always in the same form. "When the Son of Man comes in His glory, and all the holy angels with Him, then He will sit on the throne of His glory" (Matt. 25:31, NKJV). The spiritual nature of angels is the glory of angels.

While at times angels appear as radiant beings, very often angels come in the guise of ordinary men. Sometimes angels have an extraordinary likeness to humanity, whether for the purpose of testing those to whom they appear or in order to ensure that their message and purpose will not be impeded by their radiant appearance. It was as ordinary men that the two angels visited Lot and Sodom before its destruction. Lot greeted the angels with customary hospitality, seemingly unaware that they were not ordinary men (Gen. 19).

It was as an ordinary man that the angel of the Lord visited Gideon to commission him to deliver God's people (Judg. 6).

Angels have appeared to humanity in various natural forms:

- Moses in the form of a burning bush *(*Exod. 3:2, Acts 7:30, 35).
- The angel of the Lord conducted the Israelites through the wilderness by means of a cloud (Exod. 14:19).
- Angels can make their appearance in dreams, as to Joseph prior to the birth of Jesus (Matt. 1:20, 24).
- Angels can appear in visions, as to Cornelius *(Acts 10:3).*

Angels are splendid creatures, encompassed with magnificence and glory; a God-given source of strength, inspiration, and encouragement to the faithful of God. As divine ambassadors, angels are clearly placed in the intermediate realm between God and humanity. Angels are wonderful and marvelous creatures whose glory consists in their unique serviceability to the divine will of God.

> **Angels, as inhabitants of the kingdom of heaven, are spiritual beings.**

Questions:

1. Why do you believe there is a fascination with angels? _____
    _____
    _____

2. Give your personal description or impression of angels. _____
    _____
    _____

3. Give the Bible definition of angel. _____
    _____
    _____

4. Why are angels presented in God's word as dutiful servants of God?
    _____
    _____

5. Why are angels not bound by natural law that limits humans? _____
    _____
    _____

6. List the roles that angels play in human life:

    a. _____

    b. _____

    c. _____

    d. _____

    e. _____

7. Describe the role that angels play between God and man. _____
    _____
    _____

8. List some of the important events where angels have played a role for
    mankind. _____
    _____

9. How would you describe the nature of angels? _____
    _____
    _____

10. List some examples of various forms in which angels have appeared to
    mankind. _____
    _____

The Names and Titles of Angels

There is a class of beings who inhabit the vastness of the heavens. They are the angels of God; they are the tenants of the heavens. Angels have the highest habitation of all creatures. Far beyond the sun and moon are all the glorious hosts of the angels in God's presence. Jesus Christ said, *". . .angels in heaven always see the face of my father in heaven"* (Matt.18:10). Our purpose in this lesson is to examine the creation of angels, the number of angels, and the names and titles of angels.

The Creation And Home Of The Angels

The Scriptures are clear as to the existence of angels as creations of the Almighty, but the time, order, place, and manner of the creation of angels are not revealed. Thus, opinions differ as to when the heavenly beings came into existence. The Scriptures teach that God created the angels as his servants. "Praise the LORD! Praise the LORD from the heavens; Praise Him in the heights! Praise Him, all His angels For He commanded and they were created" (Psa. 148:1, 5, NASB). Psalm 148 is a most solemn and earnest call to all creatures, according to their capacity, to praise their Creator. There is, above this dark and sinful world, a world of blessed angels by whom God is praised—an innumerable company of them. All creation, from the highest to the lowest on earth, is to praise and honor its Creator for His mighty power and glory. The angels are called hosts, for their vast numbers, exquisite order, and perfect subjection to the Lord. "Thou alone art the LORD. Thou hast made the heavens, The heaven of heavens with all their host, The earth and all that is on it, The seas and all that is in them. Thou dost give life to all of them and the heavenly host bows down before Thee" (Neh. 9:6, NASB). This chapter in Nehemiah is a prayer of praise and thanksgiving to Almighty God and recognition of God's worthiness of praise from all his creation, even the heavenly host of angels.

> The angels are called hosts, for their vast numbers, exquisite order, and perfect subjection to the Lord.

It is assumed from Paul's statement in Colossians that all angels were created simultaneously. "For by Him all things were created, both in the heavens and on earth, visible and invisible, whether thrones or dominions or rulers or authorities—all things have been created by Him and for Him. And He is before all things, and in Him all things hold together" (Col. 1:16-17, NASB). Jesus Christ is the eternal Son of God and the Creator of this world. The whole of creative activity is summed up in Christ, including the angels in heaven and everything on earth.

It is assumed that the creation of the angels was completed at the time of the original creation, and that none will be added to their number. The Book of Job states that angels were with God at the time of the creation of the world as we know it today. "Where were you when I laid the foundation of the earth? Tell Me, if you have understanding, Who set its measurements, since you know? Or who stretched the line on it? On what were its bases sunk? Or who laid its cornerstone, When the morning stars sang together, And all the sons of God shouted for joy?" (Job 38:4-7, NASB).

The proper home or habitat of angels is in heaven in the presence of God Almighty. "The angel said to them,

Do not be afraid; for behold, I bring you good news of a great joy which shall be for all the people; for today in the city of David there has been born for you a Savior, who is Christ the Lord. "And this will be a sign for you: you will find a baby wrapped in cloths, and lying in a manger." And suddenly there appeared with the angel a multitude of the heavenly host praising God, and saying, "Glory to God in the highest, And on earth peace among men with whom He is pleased." And it came about when the angels had gone away from them into heaven, that the shepherds began saying to one another, "Let us go straight to Bethlehem then, and see this thing that has happened which the Lord has made known to us" (Luke 2:10-15, NASB).

The eternal God existed before the appearance of any physical world, and He encircled himself with a vast angelic host of spiritual beings far superior to man. This heavenly host was gifted with intellect, will, beauty and power far above our human level.

The Number Of Angels

The Scriptures are silent as to the exact number of angels. The Scriptures simply refer to the angels as "heavenly hosts" (Psa. 148:2). In Genesis 28:12 we read how Jacob saw the angels of God ascending and descending a ladder that reached up to heaven. Moses wrote, "The LORD came from Sinai, And dawned on them from Seir; He shone forth from Mount Paran, And He came from the midst of ten thousand holy ones; At His right hand there was flashing lightning for them" (Deut. 33:2, NASB). Daniel in his vision of God's throne said, "I watched till thrones were put in place, and the Ancient of Days was seated; His garment was white as snow, and the hair of His head was like pure wool. His throne was a fiery flame, its wheels a burning fire; A fiery stream issued and came forth from before Him. A thousand thousands ministered to Him; Ten thousand times ten thousand stood before Him. The court was seated, and the books were opened" (Dan. 7:9-10, NKJV). The Apostle John described the scene around the throne of God. "Then I looked, and I heard the voice of many angels around the throne, the living creatures, and the elders; and the number of them was ten thousand times ten thousand, and thousands of thousands" (Rev. 5:11, NKJV). Jesus Christ in Matthew 26:53 said to Peter: "Do you think that I cannot now pray to My Father, and He will provide Me with more than twelve legions of angels?" (Matt. 26:53, NKJV). The Roman legion was composed of 6,200 foot soldiers and 300 horse soldiers. Therefore, twelve legions would be 78,000 men—or angels. Our Lord's usage of the word "legion" implied an unnumbered army of angels were at his command. All these passages imply that the angels are an innumerable host of heavenly beings. "You have come to Mount Zion and to the city of the living God, the heavenly Jerusalem, to an innumerable company of angels" (Heb. 12:22, NKJV).

Angels are not subject to death or any form of extinction; therefore they do not decrease nor do they increase (Matt. 22:28-30). The angels do not multiply as does the human race.

The Names And Titles Of Angels

Angels are mentioned in thirty-four different books of the sixty-six books of the Bible. The word "angel" appears in some form, 305 times in the Bible. We are unable to identify the rank or stations of these heavenly beings. Angels being of a heavenly character and filling a divine function in God's kingdom, we would expect that they would be described under names and titles corresponding to their distinguished position. Expressive terms and names are used by God to identify his special servants.

Angel

The word "angel" implies "I dispatch, I send." These heavenly beings are referred to as angels, not to indicate their nature, but to designate their official work, as the messengers of God. Angels are employed in innumerable ways as the messengers of God for the benefit of mankind. Angels have come to reassure and offer hope to man. Angels have come to give guidance and direction to the children of God. Angels have called individuals to special missions. Angels have also rescued some of us from great dangers. Angels were very active servants of God during the Old Testament period.

Cherubim

The word "cherubim" means "to till or plough" and is expressive of diligent service. *Cherub* is the singular form of *cherubim*. The first Biblical reference to the cherubim is in association with the expulsion of Adam and Eve from the garden of Eden (Gen. 3:24). The cherubim were placed at the Garden of Eden to prevent the return of Adam and Eve into the garden. Moses placed a cherub at each end of the mercy seat in the tabernacle. The cherubim represent a new relationship of the children of Israel to God in his holiness and life-imparting presence (Exod. 25:18-20; Psa. 80:1).

Seraphim

The Hebrew word *"seraphim"* means *"the burning ones."* The plural *seraphim* is from the singular *seraph*. Some believe seraphim received their name on account of their missions to execute the fiery indignation of God upon the wicked. Others think that they are so called from their ardent zeal for the honor and glory of their Creator. The seraphim are distinguished from the cherubim in that the cherubim have four wings while the seraphim have six wings. There are seventy-three references in God's word to the cherubim, but the seraphim are only mentioned twice (Isa. 6:2, 6). The seraphim are represented in the vision of the prophet Isaiah 6:1-7. Seraphim are described as having three pairs of wings; with one pair they covered their faces (a token of humility); with the second pair they covered their feet (a token of respect); while with the third pair they flew. Seraphim celebrated the glory and honor of God Almighty and to act as a medium of communication between heaven and earth. Seraphim are God's agents for the purification of God's people.

Sons of God

The phrase *"sons of God"* indicates the close relationship that angels have to their Creator and also their interest in God's care for all creation

> Angels are not subject to death or any form of extinction; therefore they do not decrease nor do they increase.

(Job 38:4-7). The heavenly being that delivered Shadrach, Meshach, and Abed-Nego from the fiery furnace of Nebuchadnezzar was described as "the Son of God." "Look!" he answered, "I see four men loose, walking in the midst of the fire; and they are not hurt, and the form of the fourth is like the Son of God" (Dan. 3:25, NKJV).

Watchers

Daniel gives the angels in his vision the title of "watchers." "I saw in the visions of my head while on my bed, and there was a watcher, a holy one, coming down from heaven. . . . This decision is by the decree of the watchers, And the sentence by the word of the holy ones, In order that the living may know That the Most High rules in the kingdom of men. . . . And inasmuch as the king saw a watcher, a holy one, coming down from heaven" (Dan. 4:13, 17, 23, NKJV). The angels as *watchmen* are diligent in duty. They are untiringly active in administering their chosen obligations under God's directions.

There are two angels that are given a proper name in the Word of God. The first is **Gabriel**, which means *"the strength of God."* Gabriel was employed on several important missions. He seems to be the angelic prophet, an interpreter of the prophetic Word, and a revealer of the purposes of God. Gabriel flew swiftly to Daniel to inform him and give him skill and understanding of the things to come (Dan. 8:16-27; 9:21). Gabriel said to Zechariah that he was to be the father of John the Baptist (Luke 1:19). Gabriel revealed to Mary that she was to be the mother of the Savior of mankind (Luke 1:26-35).

The second is **Michael**, which means *"who is like unto God."* Michael is the only angel to be named "The Archangel." In the Old Testament Michael appears as the guardian of Daniel and the people of Israel (Dan. 10:13, 21; 12:1). In the New Testament, Michael is mentioned as contending with Satan (Jude 9; Rev. 12:7). In 1 Thessalonians 4:16 the dead will be raised and the children of God called to heaven at the *"voice of the archangel."*

God created angels as his special messengers. Angels have a definite form of organization which is adapted to the law of their being. Angels are both finite and special. They are able to approach the sphere of human life. The names and titles used by angels indicate their importance as the creatures of God.

> **The names and titles used by angels indicate their importance as the creatures of God.**

Angels and Other Created Spiritual Beings

Questions:

1. How do we know that angels have the highest habitation of all creatures?

    _____

    _____

2. Where did angels originate? _____

3. What is the proper home or habitat of angels?_____

    _____

4. How many angels are there in existence today?_____

    _____

5. Can the host of angels increase or decrease? _____

    _____

6. Explain Jesus Christ's statement in Matthew 26:53 concerning angels.

    _____

    _____

7. Describe the difference term that are used in the Bible for spiritual be-
    ings:

    a. Cherubim: _____

    b. Seraphim: _____

    c. Sons of God: _____

    d. Watchers: _____

8. What are the only two proper names given to angels and what do they
    mean? _____

    _____

9. Why did Michael contend with Satan?_____

    _____

10. Which angel will call Christian's to meet the Lord in the air?_____

    _____

Satan: The World's Greatest Enemy

The introduction of Satan in the Scriptures occurs in the third chapter of Genesis. Through the temptation that Satan set before Eve and her yielding to it, sin entered the world. Throughout the entire existence of mankind, Satan's purpose and objective has been to overthrow man as God's crowning creation and mar his happiness. Satan is hungry and eager for our souls. We need to know our enemy! The devil is subtle, deceitful, and he grasps every opportunity to destroy us spiritually. It is irresponsible to underestimate Satan and thereby invite defeat and welcome slavery.

> **Throughout the entire existence of mankind, Satan's purpose and objective has been to overthrow man as God's crowning creation and mar his happiness.**

The Names Of Satan

The names and phrases used in the Scriptures to describe Satan give us insight into his true nature:

- **Satan** — Adversary or enemy (Rev. 12:9; 1 Pet. 5:8);
- **Devil** — Accuser or slanderer of mankind (Rev. 12:9; Job 1:6-11);
- **Dragon** — Great power of destruction (Rev. 12:9);
- **Serpent** — Treachery (Rev. 12:9);
- **Tempter** — Opponent or deceiver (Matt. 4:3; 1 Thess. 3:5);
- **Prince (Ruler) of this World** — Great power and authority (John 12:31; 14:30);
- **Prince of the Power of the Air** (Eph. 2:2);
- **The god of this world** (2 Cor. 4:4).

This collection of frightful titles reveals the true nature of the Devil and supplies abundant reasons why all mankind should beware of him. It is foolishness to underestimate his power or to deny the reality of his existence.

Satan is termed "prince of the power of the air," because the air is supposed to be a region in which malicious spirits and demons dwell, all of whom are under the direction and influence of Satan, their chief. The "air" is used to represent this world (this lower region) to which the fallen angels have been banished by God Almighty. "Now when the Pharisees heard it they said, 'This fellow does not cast out demons except by Beelzebub, the ruler of the demons'" (Matt. 12:24, NKJV). The Pharisees charged Jesus Christ with being under Satan's control and authority. Satan is always pictured as the ruler of the demons and other agencies of evil. Satan does much to lead men to disobey God, and when they violate divine laws they take part with Satan against Jehovah.

Satan is also designated as the "god of this world" (2 Cor. 4:4). The name "god" is here given to Satan, not because he has all the divine characteristics of God Almighty, but because he actually has the worship of the men of this world as their god. Satan has the affections of the hearts of wicked in the same way as it is given to idols. By "this world" is meant the wicked world; or the mass of men. Satan is the god of unbelievers. Satan attempts to blind the eyes of men so they should not see the light of Gospel of Christ. Satan has domination over the world. Wicked men obey his will; they execute his plans; they further his purposes, and they are his obedient subjects. The devil has no power of his own over mankind, we may give him as much as we will; and become slaves to him as long as we please.

The Origin Of Satan

"Where did Satan come from?" is the first question raised by Satan's appearance in the Garden of Eden. Genesis chapter one describes God's creation of the material universe and its living inhabitants. But it mentions nothing about a being like Satan.

The Bible clearly indicates that God populated the spiritual realm with beings of the highest intelligence, called angels. "Praise Him, all His angels; Praise Him, all His hosts! Let them praise the name of the LORD, For He commanded and they were created. He also established them forever and ever; He made a decree which shall not pass away" (Psa. 148:1, 6, NKJV). There are two theories concerning the existence of Satan: (1) Satan was created by God as an evil influence to tempt and test mankind upon this earth; or (2) Satan was created by God as a spiritual being or angel with all the glory and honor of heaven, but he sinned against God because of pride and was therefore cast from Heaven and God's presence.

The Scriptures indicate that angels have the freedom of choice to obey or disobey God. "For if God did not spare the angels who sinned, but cast them down to hell and delivered them into chains of darkness, to be reserved for judgment" (2 Pet. 2:4, NKJV). Angels, like all of God's creation, are capable of error (Job 4:18). Neither the angels' former rank, their dignity, nor their holiness, saved them from being thrust down to torment; and if God punished them so severely, then false teachers of men should not hope to escape God's wrath. Their own freedom to choose was the cause of the angels' sin, and their sin the cause of their misery. "The angels who did not keep their proper domain, but left their own abode, He has reserved in everlasting chains under darkness for the judgment of the great day" (Jude 6, NKJV). This passage implies that angels invaded the office or dignity of another and by so doing some forfeited their own position with God. They did not continue in faithfulness, though they knew the law on which they stood. This is an example of God's severity on the fallen angels; they sinned, and kept not their first state, they fell from that state of holiness in which they were originally created; and their punishment followed, they were cast down to a place of torment, and delivered into chains of darkness, reserved unto judgment.

It appears from the Scripture that Satan was one of these fallen angels who chose to disobey God. "So the great dragon was cast out, that serpent of old, called the Devil and Satan, who deceives the whole world; he was cast to the earth, and his angels were cast out with him" (Rev. 12:9, NKJV). Jesus Christ said, "He said to them, "I saw Satan fall like lightning from heaven" (Luke 10:18, NKJV). What was the sin of Satan and when and how did the Devil fall? The answer to these questions is known only by God and Satan. Pride and ambition were probably the sins which caused Satan's fall.

> The scriptures indicate that angels have the freedom of choice to obey or disobey God.

This is sufficiently evident from Paul's warnings to Timothy about being lifted up with pride and "fall into the same condemnation as the devil" (1 Tim. 3:6, NKJV).

There is nothing in the Word of God that would cause us to believe that the loving God of the Bible would create a being specifically to do evil and tempt mankind. This theory is inconsistent with our God described in the Bible. It appears that Satan is a fallen angel that God permits to test and try mankind upon this earth (Job 1:6-12). The test and trials of Satan provide mankind the freedom of choice and the opportunity to demonstrate love and devotion to the Creator.

God is in sovereign control of His creation. Satan is a created being whose freedom of action is limited by God's will. God guards and protects His own from Satan and the evil Satan would do to them if he could. God may at times permit Satan to harass or tempt his own, but not with the intent to do them harm. Satan's motive in tempting a believer is evil: Satan wants to do harm to God's people as a way of thwarting the plan of God. Satan desires to hinder or destroy God's eternal plan for mankind. God's motive in letting Satan tempt a believer is never evil. God only permits temptation in order to bring glory to himself and to enrich the life of the believer.

The Results Of Satan's Fall
Satan became the world ruler of the spiritual kingdom of darkness (Eph. 6:10-12; 2:2).

Satan has two major powers under his control:

1. **Physical Death** (Heb. 2:14-18; 1 Cor. 15:20-26)

2. **Spiritual Death (Sin)** (Rom. 3:9-12, 23; 6:23; 1 Cor. 15:50-58).

Jesus Christ came to destroy Satan's power and offer mankind the hope of salvation.

The Nature Of Satan
Satan is not a being with horns and a tail, as is sometimes depicted; nor is he a figure to joke and laugh about. One of the devil's most effective tricks is to convince men that he does not exist.

Satan is the adversary of both God and man. Satan walks throughout the earth looking for souls to devour (Job 1:6-12; 1 Pet. 5:8). Satan accuses us to God (Job 1:6-12). Satan accuses God to man (Gen. 3:2-5).

Satan can appear as a righteous individual (2 Cor. 11:14). Satan appeared as Eve's benefactor (Gen. 3:4-5). Satan can transform himself into an angel of light (2 Cor. 11:13-15). Satan works through devices (2 Cor. 2:11): Serpent (Gen. 3); Preachers (2 Cor. 11:13-15); and Churches (Rev. 2:9; 3:9).

Satan seeks advantages. He attacks at the weakest point (Eve—alone; Christ—after fasting forty days, Matt. 4). He will attack an individual at his weakest moment as a lion attacks his prey (1 Pet. 5:8).

Satan works among God's people. Satan put it into the heart of Judas to betray Christ (John 13:2). Satan filled Ananias' heart to lie (Acts 5:3).

Satan is both a liar and a murderer (John 8:44). Satan lied to Eve and

> God is in sovereign control of His creation. Satan is a created being whose freedom of action is limited by God's will.

> One of the devil's most effective tricks is to convince men that he does not exist.

brought about the death of Adam and Eve, and the whole human race (Gen. 3:3). Satan is the instigator of all sin and evil which brings about spiritual death and separation from God (Isa. 59:1-2; Rev. 20:13-14). Satan tempts, entices, and induces men to sin.

Satan tries to deceive mankind (Rev. 12:9; 20:10; 2 Tim. 2:26). He prevents people from believing by taking the Word of God out of the hearts of men (Mark 4:15), and by blinding their minds to the truth (2 Cor. 4:4). Elymas, the sorcerer at Paphos, a servant of the devil, sought to blind the mind of Sergius Paulus (Acts 13:6-11).

Why Does God Permit Satan To Continue His Evil Work?

Satan is a free moral agent. Angels are created beings. Satan is a fallen angel. The fact that some angels sinned and were cast out indicates that angels, like men, are free moral agents, with the power to choose their own course. Thus, if God would exercise his power to force men or angels to do his will, he would destroy free moral agency, and make us mere robots. Such is not God's nature or his plan. God uses Satan in the fulfillment of his own purposes and will.

Jesus Christ is the only one who can overcome the devil. "I heard a loud voice saying in heaven, "Now salvation, and strength, and the kingdom of our God, and the power of His Christ have come, for the accuser of our brethren, who accused them before our God day and night, has been cast down. And they overcame him by the blood of the Lamb and by the word of their testimony, and they did not love their lives to the death" (Rev. 12:10-11, NKJV). We must be in Christ if we will have the victory over Satan (1 Cor. 15:50-58). "We know that whoever is born of God does not sin; but he who has been born of God keeps himself, and the wicked one does not touch him" (1 John 5:18 NKJV). We must resist the devil and he will flee from us (Eph. 4:27; Jas. 4:7; 1 Pet. 5:9). We must put on the armor of God in order to have the ability to withstand the assaults of the devil (Eph. 6:10-18).

Angels are spiritual beings that are eternal in nature. Satan, as an angel, is immune to human weaknesses such as pain, injury, sickness, or death. Indeed, he is even immune to human discomfort. There are in Satan neither parts that can be dismembered, nor possibility of corruption and decay, nor threat of a separation of parts that would result in death. God alone, by his mighty power, can destroy Satan. Satan's ultimate destination, along with all the wicked, shall be the lake of fire (Rev. 20:10). Satan and his followers will be tormented day and night forever. Each one of us has to make a choice of whom we will serve while we live upon this earth. Whom will you serve?

Satan can be resisted with the help of God.

Questions:

1. List the names and phrases that describe Satan's true nature. _____
   _____
   _____

2. Describe the two theories concerning Satan's origin. _____
   _____
   _____

3. What do you believe is Satan's origin and why do you believe it? _____
   _____
   _____

4. Why does God permit Satan to test and tempt mankind? _____
   _____

5. Does God place any limitations upon Satan's power and authority? ____
   _____

6. What two major powers are under Satan's control? _____
   _____
   _____

7. Describe the nature of Satan? What is his most destructive power? ____
   _____
   _____
   _____

8. What hope does mankind have in overcoming Satan's power? _____
   _____
   _____

9. Why does God permit Satan to continue his evil works? _____
   _____
   _____

10. What can mankind do to withstand Satan and his attacks? _____
    _____
    _____
    _____

Satan's Role in the Fall of Mankind

The Word of God begins with God Almighty creating our wonderful universe (Gen. 1). With a burst of unimaginable power God with loving care begins to form the earth from nothing. God affectionately shapes our world, forming the seas and dry land, enriching it with a collection of vegetation, and filling its skies, valleys, and seas with a vast assortment of living creatures. When God had concluded the enrichment and beautification of our earth, as the culminating act of creation, God announced his intent to create mankind. "God said, 'Let Us make man in Our image, according to Our likeness; let them have dominion over the fish of the sea, over the birds of the air, and over the cattle, over all the earth and over every creeping thing that creeps on the earth'" (Gen. 1:26, NKJV).

God Almighty, as an eternal being, is the first personality identified in the Scriptures. When man looks at the design and beauty of our earth, we can understand in a small part something of God's wisdom, love, and appreciation for his beautiful creation and for what is good. God has a very special love and appreciation for the human race.

The second and third persons introduced in the Word of God are Adam, the first man, and Eve his wife. The creation account reveals that God has unlimited power to create. God's means of creating everything in our world was His spoken word: "God said," and what He spoke came into existence. The creation of man is the exception to this rule. The Scriptures say that "God formed man." Genesis 2 says, "The LORD God formed man of the dust of the ground, and breathed into his nostrils the breath of life; and man became a living being" (Gen. 2:7, NKJV). Later, Eve is fashioned from one of Adam's ribs. "The LORD God caused a deep sleep to fall on Adam, and he slept; and He took one of his ribs, and closed up the flesh in its place. Then the rib which the LORD God had taken from man He made into a woman, and He brought her to the man" (Gen. 2:21-22, NKJV). Man is made both in the **image** and **likeness** of God (Gen. 1:26). The term "image" means that man received an eternal spirit or soul like God. How is man made in the likeness of God? Man shares the attributes of God which set him apart from other animal creations of God. Mankind has a full measure of intelligence and memory, the ability to feel, a sense of beauty, the capacity to love and be loved, the potential for creativity, the ability to choose between right and wrong, and a conscience to cause us guilt when we do what we believe is wrong. Man's true identity is not in our physical connection with the animal creation, but in the special qualities that link man to God our Creator.

Our first parents were placed in the Garden of Eden by God. In the Gar-

> **Man's true identity is not in our physical connection with the animal creation, but in the special qualities that link man to God our Creator.**

den, the peace and beauty of the whole creation were available for their enjoyment. They had the benefit of the grace and favor of God, and life was very good. Adam and Eve enjoyed a life of holiness and happiness with God. But, they were created with the power and privilege of free choice. Adam and Eve could continue to enjoy their special fellowship with God by choosing to respect and obey God's will; or they could break their fellowship by choosing to disobey God. Man was given dominion over the earth and given everything in the world for his own use and enjoyment. Adam and Eve had only one prohibition from God: "The LORD God commanded the man, saying, "Of every tree of the garden you may freely eat; but of the tree of the knowledge of good and evil you shall not eat, for in the day that you eat of it you shall surely die" (Gen. 2:16-17, NKJV).

This scene was altered by the introduction of Satan into the world. In Genesis the third chapter we have an account of the sin and misery of our first parents, the wrath and curse of God against them, the peace of the creation disturbed, and its beauty stained and sullied forever.

The best description of Satan is given by the Apostle John in Revelation 12:9:

- **Great Dragon**—Destroyer and Enemy of Man;
- **Serpent**—Treachery; Deceiver
- **Devil**—Accuser; Slanderer
- **Satan**—Adversary of God and Man

Our intention in this lesson is to examine Satan's role in the fall of Adam and Eve, and to identify the strategy he uses in tempting mankind today.

Satan Attempts to Distort Eve's View of God

The tempter was the Devil, in the shape and likeness of a serpent (John 8:44). Satan is a malignant spirit, by creation an angel of light and an immediate attendant upon God's throne, but by sin become an apostate from his first state and a rebel against God's crown and dignity. Satan is enraged against God and His glory, and envious of man and his happiness. The game which Satan chose to play was to draw Adam and Eve into sin, and by so doing to separate them from their God. Thus the Devil was from the beginning, a murderer, and the great mischief-maker. Satan intruded into the lives of Adam and Eve with the specific intention of encouraging them to sin and thus to adopt his attitude of rebellion against God. The deception of Satan is evident in his first conversation with Eve. Satan did not tell a direct lie to Eve; but led Eve to lose her faith and trust in God through half-truths and innuendos; and ultimately caused Eve to adopt his attitude toward God.

"The serpent was more cunning than any beast of the field which the LORD God had made. And he said to the woman, 'Has God indeed said, "You shall not eat of every tree of the garden"?'" (Gen. 3:1, NKJV). Eve is approached by the Devil while she is alone and at a distance from her husband, but near the forbidden tree. Satan tempted Eve so that by her he might tempt Adam. It is his policy to send temptations by hands we do not suspect, and by those that have most influence upon us. Satan questioned whether or not it was a sin, to eat of this tree. He did not disclose his design at first, but he proposed a question which seemed innocent. Satan changed the emphasis

> Satan intruded into the lives of Adam and Eve with the specific intention of encouraging them to sin and thus to adopt his attitude of rebellion against God.

from God's generosity of the freedom to eat of "every tree in the garden" to draw Eve's attention to the one tree from which she was forbidden to eat, "the tree of the knowledge of good and evil." Satan questions the kindness and goodness of God toward Adam and Eve and portrays God as oppressive and restrictive. *"Is it true that God has restricted you in using the fruits of this delightful place? This is not like one so good and kind. Surely there is some mistake."* Satan questioned whether it was a sin or not to eat of this tree, and whether really the fruit of it was forbidden. Satan's desire was to destroy Eve's faith in God, and that by their own voluntary transgressions, he could destroy Adam and Eve.

Eve's response to Satan's question shows that Satan's poison was beginning to do its work. "The woman said to the serpent, 'We may eat the fruit of the trees of the garden; but of the fruit of the tree which is in the midst of the garden, God has said, 'You shall not eat it, nor shall you touch it, lest you die'" (Gen. 3:2-3 NKJV). Eve stated that they may eat of the trees of the garden, but she left out the word "every", which emphasized God's bounty towards Adam and Eve. Eve supplemented God's original prohibition with the phrase "nor shall you touch it," which God did not say. Eve overlooked the evidence of God's love and deep concern for the first pair and had begun to adopt Satan's distorted view of God's character and actions. Satan wanted to portray God as harsh and repressive.

Satan Questions the Reliability of God's Word

The great means of safety to man is continual belief in the truth of God's declarations. Adam and Eve knew God's will. It is the technique of Satan to speak of God's law as uncertain or unreasonable, and so to draw people to sin. Satan insinuated a doubt as to Eve's interpretation of God's will. "The serpent said to the woman, 'You will **not** surely die'" (Gen. 3:4, NKJV). Satan questioned the consequences of disobedience to God's command. Satan denied that there was any danger. Satan is a liar (John 8:44). The lie has always been Satan's best method of enticement. Satan told Eve there was no danger in disobedience and rebellion against God. He said that which he knew, by his own woeful experience, to be false. Satan conceals his own misery, that he might draw men into sin and into their own ruin. Satan endeavors to shake that which he cannot overthrow, and invalidates the force of divine warnings by questioning the certainty of them; and, when once it is supposed possible that there may be falsehood or fallacy in any word of God, a door is then opened to downright unfaithfulness. Satan teaches men first to doubt and then to deny; he makes them skeptics first, and so by degrees makes them atheists. Satan's chief deception is to cause men not to fear God's warnings.

Satan Casts Doubt on God's Motives

"For God knows that in the day you eat of it your eyes will be opened, and you will be like God, knowing good and evil" (Gen. 3:5, NKJV). The Devil insinuates to Eve that God had no good purpose for her and Adam, in forbidding them this fruit: Satan is trying to create discontent with Eve's present condition. This was a great offense to God, and the highest indignity that could be done him, a reproach to his power, as if God feared his creation, and much more a reproach to his goodness, as if he hated the work of his own hands and would not want those whom he had made, to be happy. It is

> Satan conceals his own misery, that he might draw men into sin and into their own ruin.

incredible that Eve would believe that Almighty God who was so bountiful and good to Adam and Eve would forbid the provisions necessary for their happiness and comfort. The Devil intended to alienate Eve's affections from God, and so to remove her from her allegiance to God.

Satan Creates A Desire For The Forbidden

Satan suggests to Eve an attractive alternative to God's command. The Devil urges Eve to act and "to see for herself." "For God knows that in the day you eat of it your eyes will be opened, and you will be like God, knowing good and evil" (Gen. 3:5, NKJV). Satan suggests advantages by partaking of the forbidden fruit:

- **Your eyes shall be opened**—Eve would have much more of the power and pleasure of knowledge than she now possessed. Eve's understanding would be greatly enlightened and improved;

- **You shall be as gods**—Eve would be as mighty as God, not only omniscient but omnipotent also. She shall be as God himself; she shall be sovereign and no longer subject to God, self-sufficient and no longer dependent upon God."

- **You shall know good and evil**—The tree would give Eve an exalted knowledge of the natures, kinds, and origins of good and evil; and, everything that is desirable to be known.

- **In the day you eat of it**—Eve will discover a sudden and immediate change for the better. Satan could not convince Eve to run the risk of violating God's command if he had not suggested the great probability of improving herself. Satan insinuates the great improvements she will have by eating the forbidden fruit.

Satan Appeals To Eve's Pride And Her Desire To Be Independent

"When the woman saw that the tree was good for food, that it was pleasant to the eyes, and a tree desirable to make one wise, she took of its fruit and ate. She also gave to her husband with her, and he ate" (Gen. 3:6, NKJV). Satan is encouraging Eve to violate God's command and assert her independence. Eve's response to the Devil was to examine the tree. Eve chose to rely on her senses rather than on God's command.

There are three universal avenues of temptation:

- Lust of the flesh;
- Lust of the eyes
- Pride of life.

Eve saw that the forbidden tree was "good for food." The fruit smelled delicious. The fruit was "pleasant to the eyes." It looked beautiful and increased the appetite. Eve also believed that it would "make one wise." All natural and moral evil originates from these three sources. The majority of the world today still relies on their own senses rather than trusting God's written word. If something feels good or is enjoyable, man assumes that it must be good, even though God's word tells us that it is really harmful and destructive to our spiritual life. One of the Devil's consistent strategies is to get individuals to

Angels and Other Created Spiritual Beings

decide on the basis of appearances and feelings and to reject the clear moral guidance provided in the Word of God. The fact that the tree was "desirable to make one wise" was most attractive to Eve. Eve sought to be more than she had been, more than God intended her to be. Eve was desirous of independence from her loving Creator. Eve failed to realize that it is only in faithfulness to God and his will that any person can find happiness and fulfillment in this life. Eve took of the fruit and ate and gave to Adam, her husband and he ate. It does not appear that Satan tempted Adam directly. Adam received the fruit from the hand of his wife; he knew he was transgressing, he was not deceived.

The Consequences Of Doing Evil In The Sight Of God

The Hebrew word for evil is *ra'*. The group of words constructed on this root is used throughout the Old Testament to focus on two aspects of evil. As a moral term it identifies actions which violate God's purpose for created beings. As a descriptive term it used of the consequences of doing evil— the tragedy, distress, physical and emotional harm that comes as a result of wrong moral choices. What were the consequences of Adam and Eve's sin?

- **Guilt and Shame** (Gen. 3:7-8)
- **Broken Relationships** (Gen. 3:9-13)
- **Spiritual Death** (Gen. 3:22-24; Eph. 2:1-3)
- **Physical Suffering** (Gen. 3:14-19)
- **Physical Death** (Gen. 3:19; Rom. 5:12)

Adam and Eve did evil in taking and eating of the forbidden fruit and they immediately began to experience or "to know" the evil consequences of their choice.

How Can Christians Withstand Satan's Temptations?

Satan is hungry and eager for the souls of mankind today. What can a Child of God do to withstand the strategies and temptations of Satan?

- The Christian must have knowledge of God's word and let it be his daily guide.

- The Christian must maintain confidence in God's goodness and generosity toward mankind.

- The Christian must trust that God's commands are motivated by love and truly define what is best for man.

- The child of God must remember that we need not experience sin to understand its destructive properties.

- The child of God must heed the warnings provided by God in his divine word.

- The child of God must reject every temptation to act independently of God's will.

- The Christian must remember that God is Lord and that we are merely his creation.

"Submit to God. Resist the devil and he will flee from you" (Jas. 4:7, NKJV). "Be sober, be vigilant; because your adversary the devil walks about

> Jesus Christ is man's only hope of overcoming Satan and his power.

like a roaring lion, seeking whom he may devour. Resist him, steadfast in the faith, knowing that the same sufferings are experienced by your brotherhood in the world" (1 Pet. 5:8-9 NKJV).

Sin entered the world by the deliberate disobedience of Adam and Eve when they were tempted by Satan, the great spiritual enemy of God and man. Man chose to violate God's word rather than subject himself to his Creator. Adam and Eve, because of their disobedience, were driven from the Garden of Eden and from the presence of God. The future of Adam and Eve and all humanity looked exceedingly gloomy. God offered Adam and Eve and all mankind the first promise of hope in his curse upon Satan. "I will put enmity Between you and the woman, And between your seed and her Seed; He shall bruise your head, And you shall bruise His heel" (Gen. 3:1, NKJV). The promise was that the "seed of woman," Jesus Christ, would bruise or destroy the power of Satan. Jesus Christ is man's only hope of overcoming Satan and his power. Jesus Christ by his physical life and death upon the cross destroyed Satan's power over physical and spiritual death or sin. The remainder of the Bible is the unfolding of God's eternal plan for the salvation of mankind.

Satan's power over mankind was broken by Jesus Christ through His death upon the cross. Christ's victory over Satan was complete (1 Cor. 15:50-58). Jesus Christ is now glorified at the right hand of God, while Satan's power is limited. Satan will ultimately be destroyed in the lake of fire (Rev. 20:10).

QUESTIONS:

1. What does the creation of the world and mankind say about the nature of God? _____

   _____

   _____

2. How was mankind created in the "image" and "likeness" of God? _____

   _____

   _____

3. Why did God prohibit Adam and Eve from eating of the "tree of knowledge"" _____

   _____

   _____

4. Describe the nature of Satan. _____

   _____

   _____

5. Why do you believe Satan intruded into the world of Adam and Eve?

   _____

   _____

   _____

6. How does Satan attempt to distort Eve's view of God? _____

   _____

   _____

Angels and Other Created Spiritual Beings

7. Explain how Satan questions the reliability of God's word to Adam and Eve._____

_____

_____

8. How does Satan cast doubt on God's motives? _____

_____

_____

9. Summarize the process Satan used to create a desire for the forbidden.

_____

_____

_____

10. What are the three universal avenues used by Satan to tempt mankind?

_____

_____

_____

11. List the consequences of Adam and Eve's sin._____

_____

_____

_____

_____

12. How can a child of God today overcome Satan's temptations?_____

_____

_____

_____

Are People Demon Possessed Today?

> **The only safe conclusions to be reached in regard to demons are those based on the scriptures.**

The Word of God never attempts to dispute or deny the greatness of Satan's wisdom and power. Satan is termed "prince of the power of the air" because the air is supposed to be a region in which malicious spirits and demons dwell, all of whom are under the direction and influence of Satan, their chief. The Scriptures portray Satan as God's adversary who is followed by a host of angels who give allegiance to him rather than to Jehovah. Through knowledge of God's Word, and by human reasoning, and experience, we understand that there is a spiritual intelligence working in this world. Satan is a real and active personality. What role does Satan and his evil spirits or demons play in the lives of men today?

Does the Bible teach that demon possession will continue in the Christian age? An alarming number of people believe that demons are active today and that they can influence, induce or possess the lives and directly influence activities of individuals today. The belief in the existence and power of demons and evil spirits has existed among all known peoples of this world from the earliest of times. The only safe conclusions to be reached in regard to demons are those based on the Scriptures. Our purpose in this lesson is to look at what the Bible says about demons and their purpose upon this earth.

Positions Of Religious People Concerning Demon Possession

There are three major positions among religious people who believe in demon possession.

First, a number of individuals believe that demon possession as portrayed in the New Testament was nothing more than what we today call illness (physical, mental, and emotional) and suggest that Jesus only accommodated the people's superstition. Jesus Christ came to the earth as "The Word" and everything he taught was the truth from God. Jesus did not accommodate himself to the prevalent teaching of the people of his time concerning the operations of evil spirits. The New Testament writers were clear that Jesus believed in the reality and power of demons and he demonstrated his supremacy over them. Jesus Christ came *"casting out demons"* (Mark 1:39), healing those who were *"tormented with unclean spirits"* (Luke 6:18) and *"the demon-possessed"* (Matt. 4:24). It would be impossible to regard demon possession as a mere disease without doing violence to the language used in every instance of the expulsion of a demon.

Second, there are those who believe that demon possession was a reality in New Testament times and is still happening today. These individuals assume that every wicked, unusual or unexplainable act is the work of some demon or evil spirit. The proponents of modern day demon possession rely almost entirely and completely upon personal testimony to establish their case. They believe the demons can be cast out in the name of Jesus.

The third position acknowledges that demon possession was actual and real in the days of Jesus and the apostles, but is not occurring today. God allowed evil spirits and demons to assert their evil power during the time of Jesus Christ and the apostles upon the earth. God's purpose in allowing this freedom to the demons was in order that Christ could prove his power over Satan and the demons and establish the fact that he truly was the Son of God. The supreme purpose of Christ's entrance into this world was the destruction of the works of Satan and his angels. "He who sins is of the devil, for the devil has sinned from the beginning. For this purpose the Son of God was manifested, that He might destroy the works of the devil" (1 John 3:8, NKJV). One greater than Satan has appeared and by Christ's life, death and resurrection he has destroyed Satan's authority, power and evil works.

New Testament References To Demons

There are several terms and phrases used in the New Testament to identify demons and the servants of Satan:

- Demons (Mark 1:34)
- Evil spirits (Luke 7:21)
- Unclean spirits (Mark 1:27)
- Devil and his angels or servants (Matt. 25:41).

These spiritual beings are called unclean or evil spirits because they act in direct opposition to the purpose and will of God, and they attempt to pollute the spirits of men. A demon is a spiritual being that is recognized as one of the devil's agents.

The Nature Of Demons

The Gospels give us some insight into the nature of these beings called demons and unclean spirits during the New Testament period.

- Demons are spirits (Matt. 8:16; 12:43-45)
- Demons can be numerous (Mark 5:9)
- Demons seek to enter and control the lives of men (Mark 5:2-5; Luke 11:14-15)
- Demons can be unclean and violent (Matt. 8:28-31)
- Demons recognized Jesus Christ as the Son of God (Matt. 8:29; Mark 1:24)
- Demons recognized the supreme power and authority of Christ (Mark 1:27; 5:6-13)
- Demons were aware that their time on earth was limited (Matt. 8:29).

Demons, in New Testament times, had the power to speak and communicate. Jesus Christ actually communicated with demons and evil spirits and heard their replies (Mark 1:21-27; 5:1-13). Demons had intelligence and understood the implications of confronting Jesus Christ. Luke 8:28 is an example of the fear, anxiety, and torment that demons experienced as a result of Christ's presence. These facts should establish that demons are real beings and not merely ancient illnesses.

> The supreme purpose of Christ's entrance into this world was the destruction of the works of Satan and his angels.

Demons In The Old Testament

The Old Testament Scriptures show a marked unconcern with demon possession. There is no example of demon possession in the Old Testament. There are only four passages that mention demons in the Old Testament: Leviticus 17:7; Deuteronomy 32:17; 2 Chronicles 11:15; and Psalms 106:37. All of these passages are references to idolatry and the worship of pagan gods. All such activity is sinful in the sight of God. Satan is the author of idolatry. Idolatry is a violation of the covenant that the Children of Israel made with Jehovah. Jehovah is the one true God and he alone is to be worshipped.

May Demons Possess Or Afflict People Today?

Demons and evil spirits were upon the earth during the lifetime of Jesus Christ and his apostles. In the time of Jesus, individuals were helpless before the power of Satan and his demons. Jesus Christ came into the world to liberate mankind from the power and control of the Devil (Acts 10:38). The superior greatness of Christ is based upon the fact that, although Satan is powerful upon this earth, Jesus Christ is omnipotent, omniscient, and omnipresent and has all authority in Heaven and earth. "What is the exceeding greatness of His power toward us who believe, according to the working of His mighty power which He worked in Christ when He raised Him from the dead and seated Him at His right hand in the heavenly places, far above all principality and power and might and dominion, and every name that is named, not only in this age but also in that which is to come" (Eph. 1:19-21, NKJV). God has given Christ the greatest honor, dignity, power, and exalted position; from which He transacts all the affairs of His Church, and rules the universe.

Jesus Christ used his power while on earth to cast out demons (Matt. 12:22-29). Jesus declared that his power to cast out demons by the Spirit of God was a certain sign and indication of the approach and establishment of the kingdom of God (Matt. 12:28). Jesus affirms to the Pharisees that he had bound Satan and was demonstrating his domination over him by casting out demons. The purpose of both Christ's preaching and miracles was to overthrow the kingdom of Satan, as a kingdom of darkness, wickedness, and enmity to God; and to set up, upon the ruins of it, a kingdom of light, holiness, and love. Other miracles that Christ wrought proved him to be the Son of God, but his power over demons proved that he was sent by God to destroy the devil's kingdom and his works (1 John 3:8).

Jesus Christ also gave his apostles and early disciples the power to cast out demons (Luke 9:1-2; Acts 16:16-18). The preaching of Jesus and his disciples, accompanied with the casting out of demons, would result in Satan's fall (Luke 10:17-20). The seventy disciples reported that even the demons were subject to them through the name of Christ.

Christ's death and resurrection were the most grand and effectual of all means that could be used to establish the authority of Christ, break down the kingdom of Satan, and set up the Kingdom of God for all eternity. The cross was a chariot of triumph. The Scriptures teach that demon possession came to an end when Christ completed His mission and the kingdom was established and confirmed.

> Jesus declared that his power to cast out demons by the Spirit of God was a certain sign and indication of the approach and establishment of the kingdom of God.

- Genesis 3:15—*"bruise thy head"*—Christ came to the earth to destroy the power of Satan.
- Zechariah 13:1-2—*"pass out of the land"*—With the coming of Christ's kingdom *"unclean spirits"* or demons were to absent from the land.
- 3. Matthew 8:28-34—*"before the time"*—The demons realize that they had only a limited time upon this earth.
- John 12:31—*"the ruler of this world will be cast out"*—Satan's control on this earth is limited by the death of Jesus Christ.
- Colossians 2:15—*"spoiled principalities and powers"*—Christ was triumphant over all his enemies by his death upon the cross

Jesus Christ was completely successful in fulfilling God's eternal plan for the salvation of mankind. The angels of Satan have been cast into *"chains of darkness"* to await the final judgment (2 Pet. 2:4; Jude 6).

Why Is There No Demon Possession Today?

Jesus Christ has bound (limited) the power of Satan under the Gospel age. The Child of God has help and support against the wiles of the devil. "You are from God, little children, and have overcome them; because greater is He who is in you than he who is in the world" (1 John 4:4, NASB). And again, "We know that no one who is born of God sins; but He who was born of God keeps him and the evil one does not touch him" (1 John 5:18, NASB). In his conflicts with sin, temptation, and error, the Christian should never despair, for if he remains faithful God and his word, God will insure him the victory.

The Apostle Paul reveals one of God's most magnificent promises to his children in 1 Corinthians 10:13. "No temptation has overtaken you except such as is common to man; but God is faithful, who will not allow you to be tempted beyond what you are able, but with the temptation will also make the way of escape, that you may be able to bear it." This verse contains three wonderful promises from God:

- Every temptation will be such as is common to man;
- No temptation will beyond our ability to bear;
- There will always be a way of escape from the temptation.

If man's temptations were such as no one had ever endured before, and there were no way out of them, mankind might give up in despair. The temptations to which humans are subject do not require angelic powers to resist. The temptations that mankind faces today are the same that man in his human nature has faced since the beginning of time. Mankind has been provided strength and deliverance from every temptation, if man will but place his trust and confidence in Jesus Christ and His written word. Christ is man's way to victory over Satan and his temptations. God our Father will, with the temptation, make deliverance, or way out. Satan is never permitted to block up our way, without the providence of God making a way through the wall.

God does not tempt man (Jas. 1:12-18). God permits temptation; but, neither does He tempt (Jas. 1:13), nor does He infuse evil thoughts into the mind of anyone. He never creates an object of temptation to be placed in our way; but, he permits them to be placed there by others. Fortunately, Satan is limited in his power to tempt man. Mankind now has the ability to *"resist"*

> If man's temptations were such as no one had ever endured before, and there were no way out of them, mankind might give up in despair.

Satan as a result of the limitations placed upon his power (1 Pet. 5:8-9). If, then, we can resist Satan's temptations, no one can blame God or Satan for his transgressions. If men fall into sin, under the power of temptation, they only are to blame. Each individual is a free-moral agent, having the freedom to do with his life as he desires (Rom. 14:12; 2 Cor. 5:10).

Mankind is doomed to failure if he tries to engage Satan on his own ground. Man's only hope of victory over Satan is to meet him with the virtue and power of our loving Savior, Jesus Christ (1 Cor. 15:55-58).

Once Jesus Christ proved himself to be the Son of God, after the kingdom of God was established, and after the New Testament was revealed and confirmed, the demons' *"time"* was ended, and they are now confined, awaiting the judgment.

> **Mankind is doomed to failure if he tries to engage Satan on his own ground.**

Questions:

1. Describe your personal view or feeling concerning demon possession.

   _____

   _____

2. Summarize the three major positions among religious people concerning demon possession. _____

   _____

   _____

3. Describe the nature of demons as revealed in the New Testament. _____

   _____

   _____

4. Why do you believe that demons controlled the lives of those they enter?

   _____

   _____

5. Did the demons recognize Jesus Christ? _____

6. Why did the demons fear the power and authority of Jesus Christ? _____

   _____

   _____

7. Were the demons aware that they only had a limited "time" upon this earth? _____

   _____

   _____

8. Explain the use of the term "demons" in the Old Testament. _____

   _____

   _____

9. Can demons possess or afflict people today? _____

   _____

10. How did Jesus Christ prove his power over demons? _____

    _____

    _____

11. What was a sign that the Kingdom of God was near its establishment?

_____

_____

12. Why were Christ's disciples given power to cast out demons? _____

_____

_____

13. What passages of Scripture are the strongest evidence of Christ's victory over demons? _____

_____

14. What promises does the child of God have today in his battle with Satan?

_____

_____

15. If men fall into sin, who is to blame? _____

_____

Law and Order Angels:
Instruments of God's Judgment!

The angels of God are ministering spirits. Worship and ministry to God are their two-fold function. Angels are priests in the heavenly temple and messengers of God's errands of love and justice to mankind. God created the angels for a specific purpose. What they do in God's immediate presence, apart from worshipping and praising him, we are not told. But, from the earliest ages angels have been employed to make known the decrees and purposes of God concerning his dispensations of mercy to mankind.

Angelic appearances among men revealed that the function of angels was one of encouragement and care for God's faithful children. Angels transmitted God's will to individuals on earth and assisted His children in their journey through this life.

As we read the Scriptures we discover that God frequently used angels to administer justice and to punish the evildoers. Our intention in this lesson will be to examine the occasions where God used angels to execute his judgment on sinful individuals and nations.

Adam And Eve (Gen. 3:24)

"He drove the man out; and at the east of the garden of Eden He stationed the cherubim and the flaming sword which turned every direction, to guard the way to the tree of life" (Gen. 3:24, NASB). God's displeasure with the sin of Adam and Eve was evidenced by His expelling them from the paradise He had provided them. Adam and Eve were unfit to remain in the Garden of Eden because of their ingratitude toward God and their transgression of God's will. They are reluctant to leave this place of happiness. Therefore, because of Adam's unwillingness to depart their home, God drove them out.

God placed cherubim at the entrance to the Garden of Eden. These angelic beings were, for a time, employed in guarding the entrance to Paradise, and kept the way of or road to the tree of life. A detachment of cherubim, armed with a dreadful and irresistible power, represented by flaming swords which turned every way, prevented Adam and Eve from returning to the Garden.

Sodom And Gomorrah (Gen. 19:1-11)

The cities of Sodom and Gomorrah were probably located in the plain south of the Dead Sea, in southern Israel. These cities were destroyed by God as a result of fire from heaven in the time of Abraham and Lot, because of the exceeding wickedness of these cities (Gen. 13:10-13). The plain of Jordan in which these cities stood was pleasant and fruitful, like an earthy paradise; but it was first burned, and afterwards mostly overflowed by the waters of the Dead Sea (Jer. 50:40).

The crimes and vices of Sodom and Gomorrah were enormous. The sins of

> Angels transmitted God's will to individuals on earth and assisted His children in their journey through this life.

> God frequently used angels to administer justice and to punish the evildoers.

these cities were unnatural and unlawful sexual relations of men with other men or animals (Rom. 1:26-27). The modern term "sodomy" came from the nature of the individuals who lived in Sodom. The sin of sodomy was an offense against nature frequently connected with idolatrous practices.

Abraham and Lot decided to separate one from the other because of their exceeding wealth and the strife between their herdsmen (Gen. 13:6-9). Lot chose the plain of Jordon in which the cities of Sodom and Gomorrah were located. Lot was a righteous man who then found himself in the midst of an immoral cesspool (2 Pet. 2:7-8). God, because of his love and concern for Abraham, sent two angels to evaluate the cities, to execute God's purpose, and to offer deliverance to Lot and his family. Lot sat "in the gate" of the city probably in order to prevent unsuspecting travelers from being entrapped by his wicked townsmen. He waited at the gate of the city not only to transact his own business, but also to take strangers that he might encounter to his own house for protection.

The angels on this occasion appeared in human form. The angels found, upon trial, that Lot was righteous, but it did not appear that there were any more of the same character in Sodom. The men of Sodom became aware that Lot had strangers in his home. They demanded to have sexual relations with these men. The men of Sodom were intent on subjecting the two visitors to their town to homosexual rape. Lot tried unsuccessfully to dissuade them from their evil intentions. The men were obstinate and attempted to break down the door to Lot's home. The fact that every man, young and old, from every region of the city, enthusiastically joined in the attempted rape of the angels shows that Sodom was a completely corrupt society. The angels pulled Lot into the house, shut the door, and smote the men of the city with blindness. The angels, by the power which God had given them, deprived these wicked men of a proper and regular use of their sight, so that they could not find Lot's door. The following day the angels laid hold upon Lot, his wife, and two daughters, and carried them outside the city. The Lord God rained fire and brimstone from heaven on Sodom and Gomorrah (Gen. 19:24-25)

> All of these events should serve as warnings to people today, for they illustrate God's commitment to intervene in our world when righteous judgment simply cannot be put off any longer.

People Of Egypt (Psa. 78:43-51)

A terrible famine struck the Middle East, and only Egypt had a supply of food to ensure the nation of Israel's survival. Abraham's grandson, Jacob, led his small family into Egypt to escape the famine. Seventy individuals went into Egypt and there they remained for over 400 years. The majority of the time that the descendants of Abraham were in Egypt they are in the bondage of slavery to Pharaoh and the Egyptians (Exod. 1:7-14). During the time of this bondage they became a great nation of people.

God raised up his servant Moses to deliver the Israelites from Egyptian bondage. God demonstrated his power and might through the ten plagues brought upon Pharaoh and the land of Egypt (Exod. 7-12). God proved to the world that He was the only true and living God.

The children of Israel were rescued by unmistakable acts of divine power, and the Egyptians were punished for the decades of cruel oppression of God's people. The writer of Psalms details the wonders Jehovah performed "when he worked his signs in Egypt" (Psa. 78:43-51). Psalms 78:49 tells us that God "cast on them the fierceness of His anger, wrath, indignation, and trouble, by sending angels of destruction among them." It appears that God used angels to punish Egypt for their cruelty. Exodus chapter 12 suggests that angels were directly involved in the final plague upon Egypt, in which the firstborn son in every Egyptian household was killed in a single night. The Children of Israel were instructed to mark their doors with the blood of a lamb, and that when the Lord saw the blood, he would pass over that home, "and not allow the destroyer to come into your houses to strike you" (Exod. 12:23, NKJV). The destroyer is identified as "angels of destruction" in Psalms 78:49.

Children Of Israel On Their Way To The Land Of Canaan (Num. 11)

God provided safe passage for the Israelites through the Red Sea and into the wilderness of Mount Sinai, following their deliverance from Egypt. The children of Israel came to Mount Sinai to make an agreement with God Almighty to become his holy nation and chosen people (Exod. 19:3-8).

Despite all the miracles and wonders that God had performed to win their freedom and daily provided the children of Israel with food and direction, their hearts were filled with bitterness instead of gratitude, and with doubt rather than faith. The Israelites were bitter, angry and hostile toward God, despite the fact that God had demonstrated his love and care for them by daily providing a special food from heaven, called "manna." Complaints against God broke out just three days after the Israelites had been given their freedom (Exod. 15:22). The complaints continued to intensify, which led to the events in Numbers 11.

The Israelites expressed their craving for the former foods of Egypt (Num. 11:4-6). God was angered by their complaints and provided the people with a gigantic flock of quail (Num. 11:31-32). The people also received a plague from God. "But while the meat was still between their teeth, before it was chewed, the wrath of the LORD was aroused against the people, and the LORD struck the people with a very great plague" (Num. 11:33, NKJV).

The Apostle Paul in looking back on this event says, "nor complain, as some of them also complained, and were destroyed by the destroyer" (1 Cor. 10:10, NKJV). The Book of Psalms identifies the "destroying angels" as those who brought the plagues on Egypt, and also refers to this incident and says that God was angry with the children of Israel and caused their destruction (Psa. 78:27-31). "Therefore the LORD heard this and was furious; So a fire was kindled against Jacob, And anger also came up against Israel, Because they did not believe in God, And did not trust in His salvation" (Psa. 78:21-22, NKJV). It appears that there is nothing that angers God more than a rebellious individual who will not believe and trust in Jehovah and his power to save mankind.

The Nations Of The Land Of Canaan (Exod. 23:33; 33:2)

God commanded the children of Israel to exterminate and drive out all the nations of the Land of Canaan. "Hear, O Israel: You are to cross over the Jordan today, and go in to dispossess nations greater and mightier than yourself, cities great and fortified up to heaven, "a people great and tall, the

> It appears that there is nothing that angers God more than a rebellious individual who will not believe and trust in Jehovah and his power to save mankind.

descendants of the Anakim, whom you know, and of whom you heard it said, 'Who can stand before the descendants of Anak?' Therefore understand today that the LORD your God is He who goes over before you as a consuming fire. He will destroy them and bring them down before you; so you shall drive them out and destroy them quickly, as the LORD has said to you" (Deut. 9:1-3, NKJV)

How can a loving God permit such absolute destruction? The extermination of the peoples of Canaan can only be justified as a judgment from God in response to the complete corruption of their culture; just as the destruction of Sodom was a response from God for their wickedness. God promised Abraham that his seed would receive the Land of Canaan when the people's wickedness was complete. "In the fourth generation they shall return here, for the iniquity of the Amorites is not yet complete" (Gen. 15:16, NKJV.) The destruction of the Nations of Canaan was an act of divine judgment and a punishment merited because of their transgressions against God.

Two passages from the Book of Exodus clearly indicate that angels fought alongside Israel in their battles with the inhabitants of Canaan. "For My Angel will go before you and bring you in to the Amorites and the Hittites and the Perizzites and the Canaanites and the Hivites and the Jebusites; and I will cut them off" (Exod. 23:23, NKJV). "I will send My Angel before you, and I will drive out the Canaanite and the Amorite and the Hittite and the Perizzite and the Hivite and the Jebusite" (Exod. 33:2, NKJV). Angels went before God's people and assisted them in the removal and destruction of cultures whose sinful practices God hated.

Balaam (Num. 22:22-35)

The Children of Israel had completed their wilderness wanderings. They were encamped in the plains of Moab near the city of Jericho, where they continued until they passed through the Jordan River into the promised land. Balak, king of Moab, was greatly terrified of the nation of Israel (Num. 22:2-4). The Moabites entered into an alliance with the Midianites. Balak had a false notion that if he could get some prophet to pray for evil upon Israel, and to pronounce a blessing upon himself and his forces, that he would be able to defeat Israel. At the instigation of Balak, the elders of the two allied nations were sent to Balaam to induce him, by means of a bribe, to pronounce a curse on the advancing hosts of the Israelites. Nowhere is Balaam called a prophet. He is introduced as the son of Beor and as a man reputed to be of great personal power. Balaam knew the Lord, the God of the Israelites, but his knowledge was dimmed and corrupted by sorcery. "Now when Balaam saw that it pleased the LORD to bless Israel, he did not go as at other times, to seek to use sorcery" (Num. 24:1, NKJV). He knew enough about God to obey Him, yet for a long time he hoped to win God over to his own selfish plan. It is not known whether the Lord had ever spoken to Balaam before this occasion.

Balak sent some of his princes to Balaam with promises of great honor and wealth. Balaam was warned by God in a dream not to go (Num. 22:12). God laid a restraint upon Balaam, forbidding him to curse Israel. In obedience with God's command, Balaam refused to go with the elders. Quite different was the result of a second request enhanced by the higher rank of the mes-

> God does not judge sin as we do. What appears to us harmless, or at least, but a small offence, may be a great sin in the sight of God

sengers and by the more attractive promises on the part of Balak. He consults God, and is permitted to go, on certain conditions. God actually commanded him to do so, cautioning him, however, to act according to further instructions. Along the way, Balaam's donkey balked three times, which infuriated Balaam. Balaam's eyes were opened to see the Angel of the Lord standing in his way with a drawn sword ready to kill him. The Lord miraculously opened the mouth of his donkey to reprove him (Num. 22:22-35). Balaam was terrified and confessed, "I have sinned," and offered to go back home. Balaam is reproved by an angel and his own donkey for his hypocrisy and his evil desire for financial gain. When we try to compromise with temptations and refuse divine restraints, we are in great danger of being overcome by evil. Those who go against God and His word will never be successful. We have abundant proof that Balaam lived and died a wicked man, an enemy to God and His people (Num. 31:8, 16). God is present with those individuals who do not believe in God, as well as with His children. God speaks to the consciences of all human beings in an attempt to limit their evil behavior, but God does not force anyone to do what is right or pleasing in His sight.

David And The Children Of Israel (2 Sam. 24)

As King over Israel, David required Joab to take a census of Israel's fighting men, which suggests that David himself was about to rely on numbers rather than on the Lord. The pride of David's heart, was his sin in numbering of the people. He thought thereby to appear the more formidable, trusting in military might, rather than trusting only in the power God (2 Sam. 24:3). God does not judge sin as we do. What appears to us harmless, or at least, but a small offence, may be a great sin in the sight of God, who discerns the thoughts and intents of the heart.

David and the children of Israel are punished with a three-day plague. During the first day of the plague, 70,000 people died. David was given a vision of a destroying angel, with sword raised to destroy Jerusalem. "When the angel stretched out His hand over Jerusalem to destroy it, the LORD relented from the destruction, and said to the angel who was destroying the people, 'It is enough; now restrain your hand.' And the angel of the LORD was by the threshing floor of Araunah the Jebusite" (2 Sam. 24:16, NKJV). David repented of his sin and was forgiven by God.

Sennacherib And The Assyrian Army (2 Kings 19)

Sennacherib ruled as emperor over the Assyrian Empire from 704-682 BC. During his reign the army of Assyria surrounded Jerusalem and demanded immediate surrender. The Assyrians were overcome by arrogance and conceit, and ridiculed the God of Israel and bragged that King Hezekiah was powerless to save his people (2 Kings 18:17-37; Isa. 10:5-11).

King Hezekiah begged for God's intervention (2 Kings 19:1-6). In response to King Hezekiah's prayer, "the LORD sent an angel who cut down every mighty man of valor, leader, and captain in the camp of the king of Assyria. So he returned shamefaced to his own land. And when he had gone into the temple of his god, some of his own offspring struck him down with the sword there" (2 Chron. 32:21, NKJV). 2 Kings records that 185,000 men in the Assyrian army died in one night, and Sennacherib was forced to return to Assyria, where his life was taken (2 Kings 19:35-37).

Herod Agrippa I (Acts 12:20-23)

Herod Agrippa was the grandson of Herod the Great. He was set on the throne of Judea by the power of the Roman Empire. Herod sensed the hostility of the Jewish leadership toward the disciples of Jesus Christ and the church. Herod was responsible for the execution of the apostle James and the imprisonment of the apostle Peter (Acts 12:1-4).

An angel released Peter from prison before he could be killed. The angel's intervention, however, did not conclude with Peter's release. The people of Tyre and Sidon offered flattery and worship to Herod for their own personal gain. He was proud, and willing to be flattered, and even adored. He had sought their applause and had arrayed himself in a splendid manner in order to excite their admiration. When the people began to worship him as God, he did not reject the impious flattery, but listened still to their praises. Herod was willing himself to receive the worship due only to God.

Therefore, he received immediate judgment from God. God vindicated his own insulted honor by inflicting severe pains on him, and by his most awful death. He was eaten of worms. "Then immediately an angel of the Lord struck him, because he did not give glory to God. And he was eaten by worms and died" (Acts 12:2, NKJV).

All of these events should serve as warnings to people today, for they illustrate God's commitment to intervene in our world when righteous judgment simply cannot be put off any longer. Egypt was punished for oppressing God's people for decades. Cultures entrenched in evil were wiped out. Selective judgments against Israel prevented or delayed the nation of God's people from further entrance into sin. Enemies who threatened to exterminate God's people had armies destroyed. Herod Agrippa was executed by an angel when he threatened the early church. All these events were carried out by God's messengers—Angels!

Questions:

1. What was the angel's function with Adam and Eve in Genesis 3? _____
    _____

    _____

2. What was the sin of the cities of Sodom and Gomorrah? _____
    _____

    _____

3. Describe the role of the angels in the destruction of Sodom and the cities
    of the plain._____

    _____

4. What role did angels play in the plagues upon the people of Egypt? ___
    _____

    _____

5. Why did God punish the children of Israel in Numbers 11? _____
    _____

    _____

6. How could God drive the Canaanites out of their land and give it to the Israelites? _____

    _____

7. What was the power that would drive the nations from the Land of Canaan for the Israelites? _____

    _____

    _____

8. Give your personal impressions of Balaam and his character._____

    _____

    _____

9. Why does God use Balaam's donkey to reprove him?_____

    _____

    _____

10. Describe the sin of David and the children of Israel in 2 Samuel 24. ___

    _____

    _____

    _____

11. Why did God not allow Sennacherib to destroy Jerusalem? _____

    _____

    _____

12. Why was Herod Agrippa eaten of worms in Acts 12? _____

    _____

    _____

13. What lessons can we learn concerning God and his judgments from these examples? _____

    _____

    _____

Angels as God's Ambassadors:
Call To Special Service

One of the roles in which God employed angels during the Old Testament period was to call individuals to a special work or service for the Lord or God's children. Angels appeared to human beings either as ordinary men or radiant beings. When angels appeared as ordinary men, they were not always immediately recognized as angels. Angels appeared to individuals when they were asleep and when they are awake. Typically, angels appeared unexpectedly, when a person was doing something ordinary.

The purpose of this lesson is to examine the occasions where angels called individuals to a special mission. Angel encounters had a significant impact on the lives of those who experienced them. An angel encounter created faith in the Lord where none existed. Those who had faith in God and were called to a special mission found the strength to carry it to completion.

> Typically, angels appeared unexpectedly, when a person was doing something ordinary.

Abraham: Promises Renewed By Angels (Gen. 18:1-15)

God selected Abraham out of all the men of the world to be the Father of God's nation or people, through whom the Messiah or Savior would come. "Now the LORD had said to Abram: 'Get out of your country, from your family and from your father's house, to a land that I will show you. I will make you a great nation; I will bless you and make your name great; and you shall be a blessing. I will bless those who bless you, and I will curse him who curses you; and in you all the families of the earth shall be blessed'" (Gen. 12:1-3, NKJV). God promised Abraham:

* The Land of Canaan as an inheritance;
* That Abraham's seed or children would become a great nation;
* That from the lineage of Abraham, all families of the earth shall be blessed.

Abraham was chosen by God because of his faithfulness. "For I have known him, in order that he may command his children and his household after him, that they keep the way of the LORD, to do righteousness and justice, that the LORD may bring to Abraham what He has spoken to him" (Gen. 18:19, NKJV). Abraham became the Father of the children of Israel. God promised that through the "seed" or generations of Abraham, Jesus Christ the savior would come into the world for the salvation of mankind.

Abraham was seventy-five years old when he departed Haran, his home land, for the land of Canaan (Gen. 12:4). After ten years in the land of Canaan, Abraham had some concern about the fulfillment of God's promise of a son to be born to Sarah. Sarah, having no child, gave Hagar, her Egyptian maid, to Abraham and Hagar conceived and bore a son, Ishmael (Gen. 16).

God renewed his promise to Abraham and declared that Sarah was the one who would bring the promised child into the world (Gen. 17). Abraham's reaction was laughter. "Abraham fell on his face and laughed, and said in his heart, 'Shall a child be born to a man who is one hundred years old? And shall Sarah, who is ninety years old, bear a child?'" (Gen. 17:17, NKJV).

Three angels, in human appearance, came into view at Abraham's tent. It had been twenty-four years since God's original promise of a son for Abraham. Abraham invited them in to wash and refresh themselves. Sarah prepared a calf, bread, butter, and milk, for their enjoyment; and Abraham served them. The angels promised that within a year Sarah shall have a son (Gen. 18:9-10). Sarah's reaction is laughter. "Therefore Sarah laughed within herself, saying, 'After I have grown old, shall I have pleasure, my lord being old also?'" (Gen. 18:12, NKJV) The angels renewed the promise of God. "Is anything too hard for the LORD? At the appointed time I will return to you, according to the time of life, and Sarah shall have a son" (Gen. 18:14, NKJV).

> **God is always punctual to his time. Though his promised mercies come not at the time we set, they will certainly come at the time he sets, and that is the best time.**

The long anticipated son came at last. Isaac was born according to God's promise. The Lord visited Sarah in His mercy, as he had said. Isaac was born at the set time of which God had spoken (Gen. 21:1-2). God is always punctual to his time. Though his promised mercies come not at the time we set, they will certainly come at the time he sets, and that is the best time. God commanded Abraham to name his son, Isaac (laughter) for a memorial to the laughter of Abraham and Sarah (Gen. 21:3).

Jacob: Directed By Angels (Gen. 28:10-22)

Isaac and Rebekah were blessed by God with twin sons, Esau and Jacob. Later in life, Jacob, the grandson of Abraham, was fleeing from his twin brother Esau, when he had an angel encounter. God renewed to Jacob the promise he had given to Abraham and received an encouraging vision from God. He saw a ladder which reached from earth to heaven, the angels ascending and descending upon it, and God himself at the head of it (Gen. 28:12). This vision gave comfort to Jacob, assuring him that he had both a guide and a guard wherever he might wander from his father's house. He would always be in the care of God, and in the charge of the holy angels.

The Lord issued the same three promises to Jacob that he had given to Abraham. "The LORD stood above it and said: 'I am the LORD God of Abraham your father and the God of Isaac; the land on which you lie I will give to you and your descendants. Also your descendants shall be as the dust of the earth; you shall spread abroad to the west and the east, to the north and the south; and in you and in your seed all the families of the earth shall be blessed. Behold, I am with you and will keep you wherever you go, and will bring you back to this land; for I will not leave you until I have done what I have spoken to you'" (Gen. 28:13-15, NKJV).

Angels are employed as ministering spirits, to serve all the purposes and designs of God the Father. The wisdom of God is at the upper end of the ladder, directing all the actions of the angels. The angels are active spirits, continually ascending and descending; they rest not, day nor night, from service assigned to them. They ascend, to give account of what they have done, and to receive orders; and then descend, to execute the orders they have received.

Jacob labored for his father-in-law, Laban, for fourteen years. During this time Jacob was greatly blessed by God and became very wealthy. The Angel of God appeared to Jacob and told him to return to his father's homeland. "The Angel of God spoke to me in a dream, saying, 'Jacob.' And I said, 'Here I am.' "And He said, 'Lift your eyes now and see, all the rams which leap on the flocks are streaked, speckled, and gray-spotted; for I have seen all that Laban is doing to you. 'I am the God of Bethel, where you anointed the pillar and where you made a vow to Me. Now arise, get out of this land, and return to the land of your family'" (Gen. 31:11-13, NKJV).

Jacob, on his flight from home and his return to it, received guidance and protection from angels (Gen. 32:1-2). God was directing Jacob for the fulfillment of his eternal plan for the salvation of mankind.

Jacob had helped his wives and his children over the river, and he desired to be in private, and was left alone that he might fully spread his cares and fears of meeting his brother Esau before God. Jacob spent the night wrestling with an unknown person, in the form of a man. Hosea unfolds this mystery declaring the stranger to be an angel (Hos. 12:4). Jacob was blessed by the angel and has his name changed to "Israel" (Gen. 32:22-32).

Moses: Given The Law By Angels (Exod. 3)

Jacob and his twelve sons moved to Egypt to escape a great famine. Seventy individuals went into Egypt and there they would remain for over 400 years. The majority of the time that the descendants of Abraham were in Egypt, they were in the bondage of slavery to Pharaoh and the Egyptians. During this time of the bondage they became a great nation of people. The Scriptures say they became "as the stars of heaven or the sand of the sea shore." This simply means that Israel had become a great and innumerable nation, just as God had promised.

God raised up his servant Moses to deliver the Israelites from Egyptian bondage. God demonstrated his power and might through the ten plagues brought upon Pharaoh and the land of Egypt. Moses was tending the flock of his father-in-law, Jethro, at Mount Horeb. The angel of the Lord appeared to him in a burning bush (Exod. 3:1-2; Acts 7:35). Astonished at the sight, Moses turned aside to examine it. God spoke to Moses out of the fire, and declared himself to be the God of Abraham, Isaac, and Jacob. God announced his purpose of delivering the Israelites from their oppression, and of bringing them into the promised land. God commissioned Moses to go to Pharaoh, and to be the leader of the children of Israel in their deliverance from Egypt and return to the land of Canaan (Exod. 3:3-10). Moses is ordained by God to be the ruler and deliverer of the children of Israel. Moses led the children of Israel to Mount Sinai where they received the Law of Moses and became the covenant people of God. Angels assisted in the giving of the law of God to Moses (Acts 7:38, 53; Gal. 3:19; Heb. 2:2).

Joshua: Encouraged By An Angel (Josh. 5:13-15)

God commanded the children of Israel to exterminate and drive out all the nations of the Land of Canaan. "Hear, O Israel: You are to cross over

> **Jacob spent the night wrestling with an unknown person, in the form of a man. Hosea unfolds this mystery declaring the stranger to be an angel.**

the Jordan today, and go in to dispossess nations greater and mightier than yourself, cities great and fortified up to heaven, "a people great and tall, the descendants of the Anakim, whom you know, and of whom you heard it said, 'Who can stand before the descendants of Anak?' Therefore understand today that the LORD your God is He who goes over before you as a consuming fire. He will destroy them and bring them down before you; so you shall drive them out and destroy them quickly, as the LORD has said to you" (Deut. 9:1-3 NKJV). Joshua, a faithful servant of Moses was chosen by God to be the successor to Moses and the commander of the children of Israel. Joshua has superior gifts of courage, piety, wisdom, prudence and integrity. Joshua and the children of Israel were preparing to cross over the Jordon to enter into the land of Canaan and destroy the strongly fortified city of Jericho.

Joshua was awaiting divine directions as to the actual possession of Jericho, when he was confronted by the sudden appearance of a mysterious stranger, an angel who had come to assume command as "commander of the army of the Lord." God sent his angel to encourage Joshua to trust in Him and His power to deliver not only Jericho, but all of the land of Canaan into the hands of Joshua and the children of Israel. The angel appeared to Joshua in human form. God's army fought for and with Joshua and the children of Israel.

Joshua and all the generation that had served the Lord during the days of Joshua, died. Then the children of Israel revolted against the true God and served the idol gods of the Canaanites.

Each tribe of the children of Israel was given its own territory and told to drive out any Canaanites who remained. Some tribes simply failed to drive out the enemy (Judg. 1:19-21), while other tribes let the defeated enemy remain in the land in order to extract tribute or servitude as slaves (Judg. 1:35). The Lord, being angry with lack of trust and disobedience by the people, said that the "commander of the army of the Lord" would no longer fight for the children of Israel (Judg. 2:1-5). The Israelites were unable to drive the nations from the land of Canaan, without this assistance from God.

Gideon: Commissioned By An Angel (Judg. 6-7)

By worshipping idol gods, the children of Israel alienated themselves from the divine protection and blessings of God Almighty. Nowhere in the Scriptures is an individual condemned by divine justice for a crime of which he was never guilty. The idolatrous Israelites were delivered into the hands of their enemies, from whom the gods in whom they had trusted could not deliver them. National judgments upon the children of Israel may be seen in every part of the history of Israel, and particularly in the book of Judges.

The following list illustrates the Cycle of Apostasy in the book of Judges:

- Tolerance toward false religions
- Slackness in their service to God
- Plunderers allowed to destroy Israel
- Israel cries unto the God of Heaven for assistance
- The Lord hears the cries of Israel
- God has compassion of his children

- God raises up a Judge or Deliverer
- Deliverance is granted by the power of God and his judge.

In Judges chapter six it is reported that "the children of Israel did evil in the sight of the LORD. So the LORD delivered them into the hand of Midian for seven years" (Judg. 6:1, NKJV). After the Israelites turned back to the Lord, the Angel of the Lord appeared to an insignificant farmer named Gideon, who threshed a few stalks of grain in a winepress in order to hide them from the Midianites who might see him and take away the grain (Judg. 6:12). In this encounter, the angel appeared as an ordinary human being. The angel told Gideon that he had been chosen to deliver Israel from the hand of the Midianites. Gideon wondered where God's miracles of the past had gone and why He had forsaken His people. One of the greatest miracles is that God can enable weak individuals to do great things if they will obey God's will. Gideon was skeptical concerning his own abilities and the mercy of God because of the recent suffering of Israel. The angel performed a miracle to convince Gideon that God was with him and that he would be successful if he would simply follow God's plan.

Prophets: Called And Directed By Angels

There are three examples in the Old Testament where prophets of God were commissioned and directed by angels to reveal God's will to the children of Israel. When King Ahaziah, the son of Ahab and Jezebel, was injured, he sent messengers to Ekron to inquire of the false god Baal-Zebub, if he would recover (2 Kings 1:1-2). The angel of the Lord spoke to Elijah the prophet of God and told him to intercept Ahaziah's messengers and rebuke the king for looking to a pagan god for information. Elijah informs the king, "Now therefore, thus says the LORD: 'You shall not come down from the bed to which you have gone up, but you shall surely die'" (2 Kings 1:4, NKJV).

The remarkable appearance of two special angels, seraphim, in the temple in Jerusalem, changed the life of the young prophet Isaiah (Isa. 6). Isaiah heard the call of God. "I heard the voice of the Lord, saying: "Whom shall I send, and who will go for Us?" Then I said, "Here am I! Send me" (Isa. 6:8, NKJV). After his encounter with God's angels, Isaiah spent the next forty years revealing God's will to his people. The prophet Zechariah also received his teaching and direction from the angel of the Lord (Zech. 1:7-12; 3:1-8).

Our study of angel encounters reveals some of the characteristics of these spiritual beings. Angels appeared as ordinary men and as recognizably supernatural beings. Angels either delivered a message from God or called an individual to a special mission. The angelic messages revealed something about the future plans of God. Angelic encounters did not cause the individuals involved to focus their thoughts on angels, but to deepen their faith and commitment to the Lord—the one who sent the angels. God's plan for mankind was completed by these angelic ambassadors.

Questions:

1. What was the purpose of the angel's appearance to Abraham in Genesis 18? _____

_____

2. Summarize the occasions when Jacob was visited by angels.

_____

_____

3. What was the purpose of Jacob's angel encounters? _____

_____

4. Why did Moses see the angel in the burning bush? _____

_____

5. List the Scriptures that identify that angels assisted in the giving of the Law of Moses. _____

_____

6. What was the purpose of Joshua's angel encounter in Joshua 5? _____

_____

_____

7. Why were the children of Israel unable to drive all the Canaanite nations from the land? _____

_____

8. Summarize the cycle of apostasy by the children of Israel in the Book of Judges. _____

_____

_____

9. Describe Gideon's reaction to the visit by an angel. _____

_____

10. What was Elijah told to do by an angel of the Lord, and why? _____

_____

11. What was the purpose of Isaiah's call by an angel? _____

_____

_____

12. Describe Zechariah's reaction to his call to God's service. _____

_____

_____

Guardian Angels

The Word of God confirms the fact that there are two realms, the material world of man and the spiritual realm of God and the angels. Man cannot pass from the material world into the spiritual realm until death. Angels can cross into our realm and act for the benefit of mankind.

Angels, as mediators between God and man, bridge the gap between the unseen world of God and the created world inhabited by man, in order to communicate God's word and will to mankind. "For if the word spoken through angels proved steadfast, and every transgression and disobedience received a just reward, how shall we escape if we neglect so great a salvation, which at the first began to be spoken by the Lord, and was confirmed to us by those who heard Him" (Heb. 2:2-3, NKJV).

What is the God-given role of angels?

- Angels were helpers and protectors to God's people in need (Psa. 34:7; 91:11).
- Angels came to reassure God's people and to offer hope (Jesus—Matt. 4:11).
- Angels came to give man guidance and direction (The Law of Moses—Gal. 3:19).
- Angels came to call men to special missions (Moses—Burning Bush—Exod. 3)
- Angels came to rescue God's people from some great danger (Lot—Gen. 19).

Psalms 34:7 says, "The angel of Jehovah encampeth round about them that fear him, and delivereth them." Hebrews 1:14 calls angels "ministering spirits sent forth to minister for those who will inherit salvation." Many incidents reported in the Scriptures make it clear that throughout history angels have played a role in guiding and protecting God's people. The objective of this lesson is to examine the role angels have played in guiding and protecting the children of God.

> Angels, as mediators between God and man, bridge the gap between the unseen world of God and the created world inhabited by man, in order to communicate God's word and will to mankind.

Hagar: Consoled By An Angel (Gen. 16; 21:8-21)

God selected Abraham out of all the men of the world to be the Father of God's nation or people, through whom the Messiah or Savior would come (Gen. 12:1-3). Abraham was to become the Father of the nation of Israel. The fulfillment of God's promises to Abraham was obviously dependent upon his having children but Abraham and Sarah were childless. How could God keep his promise to give the land of Canaan to their descendants when Abraham and Sarah had no children? Abraham and Sarah seem to have struggled with this problem. After ten years in the land of Canaan, Sarah suggested a solution to Abraham. Sarah gave her Egyptian maid, Hagar, to Abraham as a substitute wife. Abraham could impregnate Hagar and any child she would bare would be Sarah and Abraham's child (Gen. 16:1-3). The children which were born of a slave were considered as the children of the mistress. There is no indication that Abraham or Sarah consulted God for approval of their plan. Abraham should have trusted in the promise of God, and not complied with Sarah's suggestion in taking Hagar as a wife.

Hagar became pregnant by Abraham. Hagar's pregnancy caused her to feel superior in her own judgment to Sarah her master. Hagar demonstrated contempt for Sarah. Sarah resented Hagar and her attitude (Gen. 16:4-5). The text tells us that "Sarah dealt harshly with her, she fled from her presence" (Gen. 16:6). Sarah treated Hagar so harshly that she fled into the desert in despair. The "Angel of the Lord" appeared to offer comfort and consolation to this lonely and frightened slave girl.

The angel tells Hagar to return to her mistress and be obedient to her (Gen. 16:9). The angel of the Lord promises Hagar that she will give birth to a son and that she should call his name Ishmael, which means "the Lord has heard your affliction." Hagar is promised that her son will become the father of a great nation, but the character of this nation of people would be rude, bold, untamed, and fearing no man. The Ishmaelites would live in strife and a constant state of war (Gen. 16:10-12). The Arab nation which descended from Ishmael and the nation of Israel which descended from Isaac have had continual animosity through the centuries.

The angel's directions provided Hagar the guidance she needed and she obeyed his words. Hagar returned to Sarah as commanded and gave birth to Ishmael, Abraham's son. God is concerned about the needs of all human beings and provides mankind with words of direction and guidance, if man is willing to hear and obey.

Abraham and Sarah were blessed by God with the birth of their promised son, Isaac (Gen. 21:1-7). When Isaac was born, Ishmael was filled with jealousy and envy toward Isaac. Sarah insisted that Abraham send Ishmael and his mother, Hagar, away (Gen. 21:8). Abraham resisted until God confirmed that it was His will to send Ishmael away (Gen. 21:12-13). Hagar and Ishmael wandered in the desert until their water was gone. When they were at the point of death, Hagar heard the voice of the "angel of God" calling from heaven. "The angel of God called to Hagar out of heaven, and said to her, "What ails you, Hagar? Fear not, for God has heard the voice of the lad where he is" (Gen. 21:17, NKJV). The angel renewed God's promise to Hagar and showed her a source of water nearby. Hagar and Ishmael were saved, and Ishmael became the father of the Arab peoples (Gen. 21:18-21).

Lot: Removed From Sodom (Gen. 19:12-22)

Lot was visited by two angels in the city of Sodom, who appeared as ordinary travelers. Lot offered the angels hospitality (Gen. 19:1-3). The men of Sodom gathered at Lot's home, intent on the homosexual rape of the visitors (Gen. 19:4-11). The angels revealed themselves to Lot and declared that God had sent them to Sodom to rescue Lot and his family before the fiery destruction of Sodom and the cities of the plain. Lot believed the angel's account, but was hesitant to leave the city (Gen. 19:12-15). The angels physically removed Lot and his family from Sodom. "And while he lingered, the men took hold of his hand, his wife's hand, and the hands of his two daughters, the LORD being merciful to him, and they brought him out and set him outside the city" (Gen. 19:16, NKJV). Angelic kindness surrounded Lot and his family until they were safe outside the city of Sodom. The angels were messengers of mercy on behalf of Lot and his family. Once Lot and his daughters had safely arrived in the city of Zoar, "then the LORD rained brimstone and fire on Sodom and Gomorrah, from the LORD out of the heavens" (Gen. 19:24, NKJV).

Eliezer: Guided By An Angel (Gen. 24:7)

As he nears his death, Abraham is concerned about the proper marriage of his son Isaac. Abraham calls his confidential servant, probably Eliezer (Gen. 15:2-3), and makes him swear that he will not take a wife for Isaac from among the Canaanites (Gen. 24:1-3). Eliezer is sent back to Abraham's homeland to find a wife for Isaac. Abraham expresses the strongest confidence in God, that he would guide Eliezer by his angels in finding the proper wife for Isaac, the son of promise. "The LORD God of heaven, who took me from my father's house and from the land of my family, and who spoke to me and swore to me, saying, 'To your descendants I give this land,' He will send His angel before you, and you shall take a wife for my son from there" (Gen. 24:7, NKJV). The providence of God directed Abraham's servant in his mission of finding a wife for Isaac, and in his search he had the companionship and guidance of God's angel. Rebekah willingly became the loving wife of Isaac.

Jacob: Protected By Angels (Gen. 28:10-22; 31:11-13; 32:1, 22-32)

Jehovah confirmed Jacob's inheritance of the covenant God had made with his grandfather Abraham in a dream of angels ascending and descending upon a ladder from heaven (Gen. 28:10-22). The Lord promised Jacob that he would go with Jacob and keep him wherever he might be. God also promised Jacob that he would bring him back to the land of Canaan and not leave him. "Behold, I am with you and will keep you wherever you go, and will bring you back to this land; for I will not leave you until I have done what I have spoken to you" (Gen. 28:15, NKJV). Jacob responded to God's promises by vowing to be faithful to God (Gen. 28:20-22).

The "Angel of God" spoke to Jacob in a dream and showed Jacob how to gain large flocks and herds at the expense of his father-in-law, Laban, who constantly cheated him. Jacob was reminded of his early vow to God. Jacob was commanded by the angel to return to the land of Canaan at this time (Gen. 31:11-13).

The "angels of God" met Jacob as he traveled to Canaan (Gen. 32:1). Jacob was preparing for the reunion with his brother Esau. It's important to remember that when the two brothers last saw each other, Esau's objective was to kill Jacob. The appearance of the angels was intended to encourage Jacob, who was obviously afraid, by reminding him of God's promises, presence and protection (Gen. 32:22-32).

Children Of Israel: Angels Protect The People Of God (Exod. 14:19-22; 23:20; 32:34)

The Children of Israel who were enslaved in Egypt for more than 400 years were freed by the power of God and his servant Moses. Pharaoh himself, stunned by the plagues that both devastated the land of Egypt and caused the death of his firstborn son, urged the Israelites to leave Egypt (Exod. 12:29-33; Num. 20:16). As they left Egypt, the children of Israel were guided by a cloudy, fiery pillar from God. The Israelites were guided by a pillar of cloud by day and pillar of fire by night. The different aspects allowed the children of Israel to travel both by day and night (Exod. 13:21).

Once Pharaoh realized that the children of Israel had successfully fled Egypt, he assembled an army of chariots and rushed to recapture his slaves. Pharaoh's army of chariots quickly came to the place where the Israelites had camped by the Red Sea. When the people of Israel saw Pharaoh's approaching army, they "were very afraid" (Exod. 14:10). Moses encouraged them not to be afraid. "Moses said to the people, 'Do not be afraid. Stand still, and see the salvation of the LORD, which He will accomplish for you today. For the Egyptians whom you see today, you shall see again no more forever'" (Exod. 14:13, NKJV).

The angel who had led Israel by the cloudy, fiery pillar moved from the front to the back of the camp, taking up a position between the nation of Israel and the Egyptians. The pillar of cloud facing the Egyptians blocked the light, so the Egyptians could not find a way to attack the children of Israel. The pillar gave the Israelites the light they needed to follow the path that God opened for them through the Red Sea (Exod. 14:19-20). God, in one of his most memorable miracles, saved his people from certain destruction.

Children Of Israel: Angels Gave Israel Victory In Canaan (Exod. 23:20; 32:34; Judg. 2:1)

The angels of God guided the children of Israel throughout the exodus from Egypt and the journey to the land of Canaan. Once the Israelites were prepared to enter the promised land God promised that his angels would fight for and bring victory to the children of Israel. "Behold, I send an Angel before you to keep you in the way and to bring you into the place which I have prepared" (Exod. 23:20, NKJV). Later God told Moses, "Now therefore, go, lead the people to the place of which I have spoken to you. Behold, My Angel shall go before you" (Exod. 32:34, NKJV). Following the Israelite conquest of Canaan, the Angel of the Lord spoke to the people of Israel and said, "I led you up from Egypt and brought you to the land of which I swore to your fathers; and I said, 'I will never break My covenant with you'" (Judg. 2:1, NKJV). The angels of the Lord stayed with the children of Israel and provided the daily guidance and protection they needed to keep them on the right path. God was with the Israelites and their invasion of Canaan was successful. God kept his promises, but the children of Israel failed to obey all of God's instructions and drive out all the people of the land of Canaan.

Manoah: Instructed By An Angel (Judg. 13)

The angel of the Lord appeared to the childless wife of a man named Manoah. The angel announced that the couple would be given a son, who from birth was to be devoted to the service of God. In this encounter, the angel had a radiant appearance. Manoah prayed to the Lord and said, "O my Lord, please let the Man of God whom You sent come to us again and teach us what we shall do for the child who will be born" (Judg. 13:8, NKJV). God heard the prayer of Manoah gave him and his wife instructions of how to raise their son Samson. We need to follow the example of Manoah and seek instruction and guidance from God in rearing our children. Samson would become history's strongest man. Samson who would deliver the Israelites from the afflictions suffered at the hands of the Philistines (Judg. 13:13-14). God would once again intervene in behalf of his covenant people.

Elijah: Comforted By The Angel Of The Lord (1 Kings 19:1-18; 2 Kings 1:1-17)

Elijah the prophet of God stood alone against King Ahab and his wife Jezebel who were attempting to replace the worship of Jehovah with the worship of the pagan deity Baal. In a contest on Mount Carmel, Elijah won a great victory for Jehovah over the 450 prophets of Baal. Elijah by his victory won the support of the people of Israel and convinced them that Jehovah is the only true God (1 Kings 18:15-40). When Jezebel realized that the lives of her prophets had been taken she threatened to have Elijah killed. Elijah is terrified and fled (1 Kings 19:1-3). Elijah, exhausted following a day's journey into the wilderness, collapsed and fell asleep. The Angel of the Lord woke Elijah and provided food and drink to strengthen him so he could continue his journey (1 Kings 19:4-8). Later, the Lord spoke to His despondent, depressed prophet and led him back into God's service (1 Kings 19:9-18).

The Angel of the Lord appeared a second time to Elijah and told him to pronounce God's judgment of death upon King Ahaziah, the son of Ahab and Jezebel. Despite the danger in confronting King Ahaziah, who had the power of life and death, Elijah delivered the message of God as he had been directed (2 Kings 1:1-4).

When King Ahaziah received the message from God by Elijah, he failed to repent of seeking council from the pagan god Baal instead of the one true God, Jehovah. Rather than confess his wrong, King Ahaziah sent soldiers to bring Elijah to him. The first group of fifty soldiers was consumed by fire from heaven in answer to Elijah's prayer to God, as was a second group of fifty. The captain of the third group of fifty soldiers sent to Elijah fell on his knees and begged for his life and the lives of his soldiers. The Angel of the Lord told Elijah not to be afraid, but to go and confront King Ahaziah. Elijah boldly restated God's judgment on King Ahaziah, and he died (2 Kings 1:9-17).

The Angel of the Lord gave Elijah direction when he needed it. The Angel of the Lord strengthened Elijah when he was in despair and guaranteed Elijah's safety when his mission seemed to endanger his life. God is always present for His children; and He will provide them strength when they are down. He will give them purpose when their lives seem empty, and He will protect His children when they do His will.

King Hezekiah: Jerusalem Protected From The Assyrian Army (2 Kings 19)

The Assyrian army, under the command of Sennacherib, invaded the land

> **We need to follow the example of Manoah and seek instruction and guidance from God in rearing our children.**

of Canaan and crushed all the fortified cities and easily captured the northern Kingdom of Israel. Sennacherib and the Assyrian army surrounded the city of Jerusalem and expected to easily take the city. When the Assyrian officer demanded the surrender of a defenseless Jerusalem and ridiculed the God of Israel, King Hezekiah of Judah prayed for divine intervention, and the Lord responded (2 Kings 19:3-7). The Lord sent an angel who killed 185,000 Assyrian soldiers of all ranks. Sennacherib was forced to return home, and Jerusalem and the people of God were saved (2 Kings 19:35-37).

Shadrach, Meshach, And Abed-Nego: An Angel Saves From A Fiery Furnace (Dan. 3)

The Kingdom of Judah was invaded by King Nebuchadnezzar and the Babylonian army. The Babylonians deported the upper class families and educated sons of Israel for government service in Babylon. Daniel, Shadrach, Meshach, and Abed-Nego were trained and served in the Babylonian government.

King Nebuchadnezzar of Babylon erected a golden image and required all his subjects of every rank or degree to fall down and worship the image at the sound of music which he had prepared (Dan. 3:1-7). Anyone who refused to worship the image would immediately be cast into a burning fiery furnace. Shadrach, Meshach, and Abed-Nego refused to bow down to the idol King Nebuchadnezzar had erected. King Nebuchadnezzar ridiculed the idea than any god could deliver them from the death penalty he had imposed, and they were thrown immediately into a raging fiery furnace (Dan. 3:21). The angel of God appeared and kept them safe in the flame (Dan. 3:25).

Daniel: An Angel Delivers From Harm In The Lion's Den (Dan. 6)

Daniel held high positions of honor in the Babylonian Empire and the Medio-Persian Empire which succeeded the Babylonian Empire. The princes of the Medio-Persian Empire envied Daniel and his position of power and conspired to ruin Daniel. The princes tricked King Darius into enacting a law that required that no one pray or make a request of anyone other than the King for thirty days (Dan. 6:4-9). Daniel continued to pray three times each day by his open window to the God of Heaven. The princes accused Daniel of violating the law of the King, and Darius reluctantly ordered that Daniel be thrown into a den of hungry lions (Dan. 6:10-15). Darius, who respected and liked Daniel, expressed his hope that: "Your God, whom you serve continually, He will deliver you" (Dan. 6:16, NKJV). The next morning Daniel emerged alive and well. "My God sent His angel and shut the lions' mouths, so that they have not hurt me, because I was found innocent before Him; and also, O king, I have done no wrong before you" (Dan. 6:22, NKJV.

A review of these incidents reveals the following characteristics of angel guidance:

- Guidance was most frequently provided for individuals who did not know what to do (Hagar, Jacob, Samson's parents).
- Guidance was direction from God and always explicit and clear.
- Guidance from God is always the best way to proceed (Gen. 21:17). God cares about his children and will always provide the proper guidance and protection.

Questions:

1. What is the God-given role of angels? _____
    _____

2. Does God promise that angels will guide and protect his children? ____

3. Who is Hagar and what is her connect with Abraham and Sarah? _____
    _____

4. Describe the angel encounters of Hagar. _____
    _____

5. What promise does God make to Hagar concerning her son, Ishmael?
    _____

6. What was the process by which the angels delivered Lot and his family
    from Sodom? _____
    _____

7. Why did God send an angel to guide Abraham's servant in finding a wife
    for Isaac? _____
    _____

8. How did God through angels guide and protect Jacob from both Laban
    and Esau? _____
    _____

9. What guidance and protection did God provide for Israel in their exodus
    from Egypt? _____
    _____

10. Who fought for Israel in the conquest of the land of Canaan?_____
    _____

11. Why did the angel of the Lord appear to Manoah and his wife? _____
    _____

12. How did God answer the prayer of King Hezekiah? _____
    _____

13. Why did Shadrach, Meshach, and Abed-Nego refuse to worship the
    golden image of King Nebuchadnezzar? _____
    _____

14. Why was Daniel placed in the den of lions? _____
    _____

15. What lessons can we learn concerning God's care for his children in
    these stories?_____
    _____

New Testament Teachings Concerning Angels

Jesus Christ came to this world to reveal God's will and purpose unto mankind. During his earthly ministry, Jesus taught extensively concerning angels. The apostolic writers also made mention on occasions concerning the role of angels in completing God's plan. Our purpose in this lesson is to examine these New Testament teachings concerning these angelic beings and see what God wants us to know.

Jesus Christ's Teachings Concerning Angels

Jesus Christ taught that angels do not have normal human characteristics. Yet at times they did appear in human form in the guise of ordinary men. Angels are neither human nor ordinary men. Angels are eternal spiritual beings, and they are not subject to physical death. Jesus stated that when mankind is resurrected from the dead he will be equal to the angels. "Nor can they die anymore, for they are equal to the angels and are sons of God, being sons of the resurrection" (Luke 20:36, NKJV). In the Old Testament the phrase "sons of God" was used to identify angels as members of a class of beings created directly by the hand of God. There is neither birth nor death among angels. Angels have continued to exist since the beginning of their creation, they do not die. The child of God has no reason to fear death, because at the resurrection, they will become like angels, no longer subject to death.

Jesus Christ also stated that angels do not marry. "Jesus answered and said to them, 'You are mistaken, not knowing the Scriptures nor the power of God. For in the resurrection they neither marry nor are given in marriage, but are like angels of God in heaven'" (Matt. 22:29-30, NKJV; cf. Mark 12:25). Angels do not procreate, so the institution of marriage does not apply. The indication from the Word of God is that angels are sexless, they are not male or female. The angel encounters in which angels appear as ordinary human beings, they are always referred to as "men." Life in heaven will not be like life on earth.

Jesus Christ affirmed that the proper home or habitat of angels is in heaven in the presence of God Almighty. "I say to you, whoever confesses Me before men, him the Son of Man also will confess before the angels of God. But he who denies Me before men will be denied before the angels of God" (Luke 12:8-9, NKJV). As inhabitants of the spiritual realm, angels have experienced the direct presence of God. Angels know God in ways that mankind does not. Angels have free moral agency and can sin and leave their proper habitation with God. "Then He will also say to those on the left hand, 'Depart from Me, you cursed, into the everlasting fire prepared for the devil and his angels'" (Matt. 25:41). The angels who left their proper habitat are

> **The child of God has no reason to fear death, because at the resurrection, they will become like angels, no longer subject to death.**

"reserved in everlasting chains under darkness for the judgment of the great day" (Jude 6, NKJV; cf. 2 Pet. 2:4).

Angels are interested in, and concerned about men upon this earth. Jesus Christ taught that angels rejoice over the repentance of any sinner. "I say to you, there is joy in the presence of the angels of God over one sinner who repents" (Luke 15:10, NKJV). Angels take an interest in the welfare of God's children. "Take heed that you do not despise one of these little ones, for I say to you that in heaven their angels always see the face of My Father who is in heaven" (Matt. 18:10, NKJV). Jesus Christ does not state that every individual has a guardian angel, but that the angels were, in general, the guardians and protectors of God's children and aided them, and watched over them (Heb. 1:14). The context of the passage is dealing with offending or causing the fall of one of God's children. The child of God needs to show love and concern for every child of God, because God is concerned about each and every one of his children. The Father takes special care of his "little ones" or his children. Angels were always ready to respond should God send them to the aid of one of his children. Jesus taught that He could receive divine protection from the angels, if He desired (Matt. 26:53). Angels carry or aid the dead in entrance into the Hadean realm (Luke 16:22).

Jesus spoke of angels being involved at history's conclusion. Angels have served as God's agents of justice throughout history, and as history draws to a close, angels will gather "the wicked" for final punishment. "The Son of Man will send out His angels, and they will gather out of His kingdom all things that offend, and those who practice lawlessness" (Matt. 13:41 NKJV). Angels will also gather the elect for eternal salvation upon Christ's return. "He will send His angels with a great sound of a trumpet, and they will gather together His elect from the four winds, from one end of heaven to the other" (Matt. 24:31, NKJV; cf. Mark 13:27). The angels do not know the time of Christ's return, only the Father knows. "But of that day and hour no one knows, not even the angels of heaven, but My Father only" (Matt. 24:36, NKJV cf. Mark 13:32). Jesus Christ will return in the company of God's angels. "When the Son of Man comes in His glory, and all the holy angels with Him, then He will sit on the throne of His glory" (Matt. 25:31, NKJV). Jesus Christ will come personally, in the glory of the Father, accompanied by all the holy angels.

Jesus Christ uses angels to symbolize the new revelation of God's will to mankind. "He said to him, 'Most assuredly, I say to you, hereafter you shall see heaven open, and the angels of God ascending and descending upon the Son of Man'" (John 1:51, NKJV). A clear and abundant revelation of God's will is now available unto all mankind. Heaven itself has been laid open, and all the mysteries relative to salvation and glorification of man have now been fully revealed. The angels of God ascending and descending is to be understood as continuous communication that is now open between heaven and earth through the medium of Jesus Christ and his revealed word. Jesus Christ is the perfect ambassador or mediator between God and mankind. The angels were God's agents by which he often expressed his will to mankind. Jesus Christ is God's only spokesman today. Angels did not know God's plan until it was revealed to the apostles (1 Pet. 1:12).

> Angels take an interest in the welfare of God's children.

> Jesus Christ will return in the company of God's angels.

The Apostolic Teachings Concerning Angels

Stephen stated that angels were present at the presentation of the Law of Moses to the nation of Israel. "This is he who was in the congregation in the wilderness with the Angel who spoke to him on Mount Sinai, and with our fathers, the one who received the living oracles to give to us" (Acts 7:38, NKJV). Stephen also stated that the Israelites "received the law by the direction of angels" (Acts 7:53).

The Apostle Paul confirmed that angels were present at the giving of the Law of Moses to the nation of Israel. "What purpose then does the law serve? It was added because of transgressions, till the Seed should come to whom the promise was made; and it was appointed through angels by the hand of a mediator" (Gal. 3:19, NKJV; cf. Heb. 2:2).

The Apostle Paul states that "we shall judge angels" (1 Cor. 6:3). The Apostle Paul is reproving the Corinthians for going to law against a brother in Christ before heathen or unbelieving judges. Paul emphasized that Christians should be able to settle their differences and disagreement among themselves, and not expose Christianity to contempt in the eyes of the men of this world (1 Cor. 6:1-2). Christians will not judge angels or anyone else. All judgment will belong to Jesus Christ. There is no account that angels will undergo a trial or judgment. Christians will be qualified to see the justice of even the sentence which is pronounced on the fallen angels, because of their knowledge of the gospel of Christ.

It is possible that angels are witnesses at the assemblies of the saints in worship to God (1 Cor. 11:10). It appears that the angels of God are interested in the affairs of God's children and are sometimes present in our worship assemblies. Angels observed the work and success of the apostles of Jesus Christ (1 Cor. 4:9).

Angels are a higher rank or order than mankind. "What is man that You are mindful of him, Or the son of man that You take care of him? You have made him a little lower than the angels; You have crowned him with glory and honor, And set him over the works of Your hands" (Heb. 2:6-7, NKJV). The Apostle Peter said that angels were "greater in power and might" than mankind (2 Pet. 2:11). The Hebrew writer says that when Jesus Christ came to earth and took upon himself a human form that he was made "a little lower than the angels" (Heb. 2:9).

Paul taught that no man is to offer worship to an angel (Col. 2:18). All forms of worship are to be directed to God only. The Book of Revelation records the Apostle John's attempts to worship an angel. "I fell at his feet to worship him. But he said to me, 'See that you do not do that! I am your fellow servant, and of your brethren who have the testimony of Jesus. Worship God! For the testimony of Jesus is the spirit of prophecy'" (Rev. 19:10, NKJV). "Now I, John, saw and heard these things. And when I heard and saw, I fell down to worship before the feet of the angel who showed me these things. Then he said to me, 'See that you do not do that. For I am your fellow servant, and of your brethren the prophets, and of those who keep the words of this book. Worship God'" (Rev. 22:8-9, NKJV).

Angels lead all creation in their praise and worship of God. Nowhere is

> It appears that the angels of God are interested in the affairs of God's children and are sometimes present in our worship assemblies.

their service to God rendered more perfectly than in their prostration and worship before the divine throne of God. "All the angels stood around the throne and the elders and the four living creatures, and fell on their faces before the throne and worshiped God, saying: 'Amen! Blessing and glory and wisdom, Thanksgiving and honor and power and might, Be to our God forever and ever. Amen'" (Rev 7:11-12, NKJV). The Book of Revelation portrays angels as active servants of God.

The Apostle Paul stated that Jesus Christ's second coming will be declared "with the voice of an archangel" (1 Thess. 4:16). Jesus Christ will return to execute his judgment upon all mankind in the company of his holy angels. "The Lord Jesus is revealed from heaven with His mighty angels, in flaming fire taking vengeance on those who do not know God, and on those who do not obey the gospel of our Lord Jesus Christ" (2 Thess. 1:7-8, NKJV).

Christ's Relationship To Angels (Heb. 1:1-14)

The Gospel writers seem to assume that Christ is superior to angels, but the exact relationship between Jesus and angels is clearly revealed in the book of Hebrews. The writer of Hebrews demonstrates that Jesus Christ is superior to angels in every way. The following list contrasts Jesus Christ and the angels:

1. Jesus Christ is a unique individual (Heb. 1:1-3).

- Jesus is "heir of all things." Jesus, as the Son of God, holds rightful title to the universe and all it contains. Christ has been given all authority in heaven and earth.

- Jesus is the one "through whom also He (God) made the worlds." Jesus Christ assisted God the Father in the creation of the world and mankind. Jesus is the master of times past, who from the beginning has guided all things toward God's intended conclusion.

- Jesus is "the brightness of His (God's) glory." Jesus was on equality with God the Father before coming to the earth. Jesus shines with God's own glory.

- Jesus is the "express image of His (God's) person." Jesus bears the stamp of God's essential nature. Jesus as the Son of God has the qualities of God the Father.

- Jesus is "upholding all things by the word of His power." The very existence of natural law depends on the active involvement of the Son of God. Christ upholds and supports all things upon this earth.

- Jesus "purged our sins." Jesus shed his own blood for the sins of mankind. Jesus has shown concern for mankind by personally cleansing us of our sins.

- Jesus "sat down at the right hand of the Majesty on high." Christ's redemptive work being complete, He has been restored to his original glory and is now at the right hand of God in Heaven.

- No angel is equal to Christ!

2. God never acknowledged any angel as "My Son" (Heb. 1:5-7).

> The scriptures make it readily apparent that Christ is far superior to the angels.

The Hebrew writer quotes Messianic texts from the Old Testament which identify the Messiah (Christ) as God's son. Jesus Christ, as firstborn, has the standing of heir to the entire universe. The Old Testament speaks of angels as worshiping Christ, and it describes angels as "ministers of flame" under Christ's control. The Scriptures make it readily apparent that Christ is far superior to the angels.

3. God never invited angels to rule his universe (Heb. 1:8-14).

The writer of Hebrews quotes the Old Testament again, this time the Messianic Psalms, to show that God called his Son to the throne of the universe, which he created and which is the eternal kingdom. God never said to an angel: "Sit at my right hand." Instead, he called angels "ministering spirits" and sent them to minister to the human beings who will inherit salvation. Angels cannot compare to Jesus Christ in identity, glory, status, or role in God's universe.

In Hebrews 2:1-3, the writer issues a warning: since Christ is so much greater than the angels, the revelation given in Christ must be far greater than the revelation given through angels, and it surely must not be neglected.

Jesus Christ's teachings concerning angels reaffirm that angels were ministering spirits sent to help Christ complete God's plan of salvation for mankind. Jesus Christ is superior to the angels and he is our guide to salvation today!

Questions:

1. Summarize the nature of angels from the teachings of Jesus Christ._____
    _____
    _____
    _____

2. Can the number of angels increase or decrease? Give a reason for your answer. _____
    _____
    _____

3. What is the proper home or habitat of angels?_____
    _____
    _____

4. Can angels sin or do those things that are contrary to God's will? _____
    _____

5. How do we know that angels are interested in the welfare of individuals upon earth? _____
    _____

6. Do you believe that each individual has a personal guardian angel?____

7. Explain how the angels will serve as God's agents of justice at the end of time. _____
    _____
    _____

8. Why do you believe the angels will accompany Christ upon his return?

_____

_____

9. Who is God's spokesman for mankind today?_____

10. What part did angels play in the giving and receiving of the Law of Moses? _____

_____

11. How can Christians judge angels? _____

_____

12. What is the rank of mankind in relation to angels? _____

_____

13. Do you believe angels are present in the assembly of the saints? Why?

_____

_____

14. Why do you believe we are forbidden to worship angels?_____

_____

15. How does the Book of Revelation portray the role of angels today?____

_____

_____

16. Contrast the relationship between Jesus Christ and angels from Hebrews 1.

_____

_____

_____

_____

Angels in the Life of Jesus

> The angel Gabriel described the role that Jesus would fulfill while upon earth, summarizing in a few words the major themes developed in the Old Testament prophecies concerning the promise.

Most individuals are unaware of the significant role angels played during the earthly life of Jesus Christ. At each stage of Jesus' sojourn on earth, angels were involved. Our intention in this lesson is to study the occasions where angels aided, comforted, and provided Jesus Christ whatever was necessary for the completion of his work on earth.

The Angel Gabriel Announced the Birth of John the Baptist (Luke 1:5-25)

Zacharias was a priest of the tribe of Levi. Zacharias and his wife, Elizabeth, was a righteous couple who had no children (Luke 1:6). The birth of a son was humanly impossible because "they both were well advanced in years" (Luke 1:7). However, with God all things are possible. Zacharias was offering incense in the temple of the Lord when an angel of the Lord appeared to him. "When Zacharias saw him, he was troubled, and fear fell upon him" (Luke 1:12, NKJV). The angel announced that Zacharias and Elizabeth would soon have a son, who was to be called John. The angel told Zacharias that his son would prepare the way for the coming Messiah or Christ, the savior of Israel and the world. "He will turn many of the children of Israel to the Lord their God. He will also go before Him in the spirit and power of Elijah, 'to turn the hearts of the fathers to the children,' and the disobedient to the wisdom of the just, to make ready a people prepared for the Lord" (Luke 1:16-17, NKJV; cf. Mal. 4:5-6). Zacharias' response was one of doubt (Luke 1:18).

The angel identified himself as Gabriel, one "who stands in the presence of God," who was sent by God to speak to Zacharias and bring him the good news (Luke 1:19). Gabriel declares to Zacharias that because he failed to believe in the power of God, Zacharias would be mute until the birth of his son, John the Baptist. Zacharias' son John was to be the "forerunner" or the "advance man" for the Lord Jesus Christ to turn the hearts of the people back to God.

The Angel Gabriel Announced the Birth of Jesus Christ (Luke 1:26-38)

Six months after Elizabeth became pregnant with John, the angel Gabriel appeared to a young virgin named Mary, to announce the birth of the world's savior. The infinite wisdom of God arranged the entire plan for the coming of the Messiah into the world. Mary was unafraid at the appearance of the angel Gabriel, but was troubled by his greeting. "Rejoice, highly favored one, the Lord is with you; blessed are you among women" (Luke 1:28, NKJV). Mary was highly favored being chosen in preference to all the women upon earth, to be the mother of the long awaited Messiah or Savior of the world.

Gabriel announced to Mary that she would conceive and give birth to a child, who was to be called "Jesus" (Luke 1:31-33). The angel Gabriel described the role that Jesus would fulfill while upon earth, summarizing in a few words the major themes developed in the Old Testament prophecies concerning the promised Messiah.

Messiah—Christ—"The Anointed One"

1. **"Call his name 'Jesus'"**—The name Jesus means salvation is of Jehovah. Jesus came to save the world from sin (Matt. 1:21).

2. **"He will be great"**—Christ was given all power and authority by God both in Heaven and in earth (Matt. 28:18; Eph. 1:20-21). Jesus Christ was wonderful and mighty in both deeds and words while upon this earth (Isa. 9:6).

3. **"The Son of the Highest"**—Christ is the Son of God. Jesus is Immanuel, "God with us" (Isa. 7:14). The Son of God left His place with God the Father and came to earth in the form of human flesh (Phil. 2:5-8).

4. **"The Lord God will give him the throne of his father David"**—Jesus Christ would be the eternal head and king over God's kingdom i.e., over the people of God, which is the church today (2 Sam. 7:12; Psa. 132:11; Isa. 9:6-7).

5. **"He will reign over the house of Jacob forever and of His Kingdom there will be no end"**—Jesus Christ is King of kings and Lord of lords. He is the ruler over the children of God and there will be no end to His kingdom (Dan. 2:44; 7:14, 27).

Mary demonstrated great trust and confidence in the angel's message, but she did wonder how she could become pregnant, in view of the fact that she had never had sexual relations with a man (Luke 1:34). Gabriel explained that she would be overshadowed by the Holy Spirit, enabling her to give birth without the implanting of human seed, so the child would be called the "Son of God."

Mary's response to the angel Gabriel's announcement was remarkable. "Then Mary said, 'Behold the maidservant of the Lord! Let it be to me according to your word'" (Luke 1:38, NKJV). Mary did not have Zacharias' unbelief. There was no concern about what Joseph would do, or what her family and friends would think or say. Mary's trust and confidence in God and her willingness to obey are examples for us all. The angel Gabriel played a significant role in preparing the world for the Savior's birth and mankind's understanding of who Jesus was.

Angels Encouraged Joseph to Go Through With the Marriage to Mary (Matt. 1:18-25)

The birth of Jesus Christ was not in the ordinary and natural way, but His mother Mary was found to be with child by the extraordinary and miraculous operation of the Holy Ghost.

Joseph and Mary were "betrothed" for marriage. Betrothal with the ancient Hebrews was of a more formal and far more binding nature than the "engagement" is with us today. The Jews were usually betrothed ten or twelve months prior to the marriage. So sacred was this relationship that unfaithfulness to it was deemed adultery, and was punishable by death – death by stoning (Deut. 22:23-28). Those betrothed were regarded as husband and wife, and could only be separated by divorcement.

When Joseph learned that Mary was pregnant before they had consummated their marriage, he quietly decided to put Mary away privately. An angel of the Lord appeared to Joseph in a dream and told him, "Joseph, son of David, do not be afraid to take to you Mary your wife, for that which is conceived in her is of the Holy Spirit" (Matt. 1:20, NKJV). The angelic message was a command to Joseph to complete the marriage ceremony at once. This command from God was to protect the reputation of Mary as well as her child. Joseph obeyed as the angel commanded him. Jesus was to be raised by parents whose lives exemplified faith and trust in God.

Angels Announced Jesus Christ's Entry Into The World (Luke 2:8-15)

Shepherds tending their flock near the city of Bethlehem experienced an angel encounter on the night of Christ's birth. The first announcement of His birth was made to shepherds, Jesus himself being the chief Shepherd, and the true Shepherd (John 10:11). An angel came in glorious appearance, probably an extraordinary light, for it is said, "it shone round about them" (Luke 2:9). The shepherds were afraid, but the angel reassured the shepherds and told them: "I bring you good tidings of great joy which will be to all people. For there is born to you this day in the city of David a Savior, who is Christ the Lord" (Luke 2:10-11, NKJV). The way to salvation and peace with God was about to be made available to all mankind through the Gospel of Christ. The knowledge of God's word was no longer to be confined to the children of Israel, but was to be offered to the entire world.

The angel of the Lord was joined by a multitude of the heavenly host, praising God. "Glory to God in the highest, and on earth peace, goodwill toward men" (Luke 2:14, NKJV). God should receive the glory and honor of all mankind for God's good-will toward men. God manifested His love for mankind in sending the Messiah, or the Christ, to redeem the world from the bondage of sin. The coming of Christ brought the opportunity for peace with God for all mankind through the Gospel of Jesus Christ.

Joseph Was Warned By An Angel To Leave Bethlehem And Go To Egypt (Matt. 2:13-15)

Angels guarded Jesus during his early years. After the birth of Christ, wise men from the East came to Jerusalem to worship the Savior of the world and the new "King of the Jews" (Matt. 2:1-2). The wise men inquired of King Herod as to the place of Christ's birth. They are directed by the chief priests and scribes to Bethlehem (Matt. 2:3-11). Subsequently the wise men were "divinely warned in a dream that they should not return to Herod" or to Jerusalem (Matt. 2:12). God warned the wise men to go home another way. No angels are mentioned on this occasion, but it is possible that an angel delivered this message to the wise men. King Herod, feeling threatened by the birth of Jesus, had "all the male children who were in Bethlehem and in all its districts, from two years old and under" put to death (Matt. 2:16, NKJV).

> The knowledge of God's word was no longer to be confined to the children of Israel, but was to be offered to the entire world.

> God manifested His love for mankind in sending the Messiah, or the Christ, to redeem the world from the bondage of sin.

Following the visit of the wise men, Joseph is directed by the angel of the Lord in a dream to take his young family and flee from Bethlehem to Egypt. No sooner had Joseph and Mary departed than Herod sent soldiers to murder every male child under two years of age. Joseph, Mary and Jesus remained in Egypt until the death of Herod (Matt. 2:13-15). This is the only time that Jesus was outside the nation of Israel.

An Angel Told Joseph When It Was Safe To Return To Israel (Matt. 2:19-23)

Following King Herod's death in approximately 4 B.C., an angel told Joseph that it was safe to return to Israel. Matthew records that Joseph was "warned by God in a dream" to go to the city of Nazareth in Galilee rather than to return to Judea (Matt. 2:22). God had sent Joseph into Egypt, and there he stayed until God ordered him back to Israel. This event illustrates that when the child of God is obedient to God's will, he will always be cared for and prosper.

Angels Ministered To Jesus Following His Temptation (Matt. 4:1-11)

As He began His earthly ministry, Jesus was led by the Holy Spirit into the desert to be tempted of the Devil. Thus the first act of the ministry of Jesus Christ was a confrontation with Satan. Christ was tempted in all manner of ways by Satan, and still overcame, that mankind also through the power of Christ and the gospel may overcome the temptations of the Devil (Heb. 4:14-16). The grand purpose of Christ's coming to the earth was to destroy Satan's power and rescue mankind from the dominion of Satan. Christ had to be tempted because:

- It was impossible that the one who came to overthrow the kingdom of Satan should not be attacked by the great adversary at the very beginning.

- The faithfulness of Jesus Christ had to be tested or proved.

- Christ by being tempted like all mankind, and yet gaining the victory over Satan is able to give "aid" to those who are tempted (Heb. 2:18).

- Christ had to set an example for mankind of how to overcome the temptation of Satan.

Jesus fasted for forty days before his struggle with Satan. The forty day fast would obviously physically weaken Christ. Jesus Christ met every challenge of the Devil but was exhausted afterward. "Then the devil left Him, and behold, angels came and ministered to Him" (Matt. 4:11, NKJV). Matthew does not reveal exactly what the angels did, but they surely supplied His needs, and comforted Him.

Angels Ministered To Jesus In The Garden Of Gethsemane (Luke 22:43)

Jesus experienced intense mental and emotional stress in the Garden of Gethsemane the night before his crucifixion. Christ, as a man who is about to suffer the cruel and shameful death upon the cross, had a terrible conflict between the horror and fear of death by crucifixion, and His desire to be obedient to God's will and purpose. Jesus said, "My soul is exceedingly sorrowful, even to death" (Matt. 26:38, NKJV). Christ's prayer in the garden is for strength to fulfill God's eternal plan and purpose for mankind. Luke records the agony of our Lord: "And being in agony, He prayed more earnestly. Then His sweat became like great drops of blood falling down to the ground" (Luke 22:44, NKJV). An angel from heaven appeared to Jesus in His moment of distress to strengthen Him. Jesus Christ was the Son of God, but also humanity. His miracles sufficiently attested to His divinity; but His hunger, weariness, and agony in the garden, as well as His death and burial, were also proof of his humanity. As a man, he needed the assistance of an angel to support His body, worn down by fatigue and suffering.

An Angel Rolled Away The Stone That Sealed Jesus' Tomb (Matt. 28:1-2)

Jesus had been crucified and His body placed in the tomb of a rich man, Joseph from Arimathea. The tomb was sealed by rolling a rounded, heavy stone along a track cut into the rock tomb. Some of Christ's disciples came to the tomb early on Sunday morning, intending to anoint the body of Jesus with spices. These disciples were woman and they were concerned about how they would be able to roll away the heavy stone from the sealed tomb.

"Mary Magdalene and the other Mary came to see the tomb. And behold, there was a great earthquake; for an angel of the Lord descended from heaven, and came and rolled back the stone from the door, and sat on it" (Matt. 28:2, NKJV). No angel was necessary to unseal the tomb and release Jesus, for he had already risen and departed. The angel was sent for the sake of the disciples of Jesus who would visit the tomb and find it empty.

Angels Announced The Resurrection Of Jesus Christ (Matt. 28:3-5; Mark 16:5-7; Luke 24:4-8; John 20:11-16)

Angels had the privilege of being the first to announce the resurrection of Jesus Christ. In each of the encounters with the angels following the resurrection of Christ, the same basic message was shared with the disciples of Christ:

- The angel answered and said to the women, "Do not be afraid, for I know that you seek Jesus who was crucified. He is not here; for He is risen, as He said. Come, see the place where the Lord lay" (Matt. 28:5-6, NKJV)

- He said to them, "Do not be alarmed. You seek Jesus of Nazareth, who was crucified. He is risen! He is not here. See the place where they laid Him" (Mark 16:6, NKJV)

- Then, as they were afraid and bowed their faces to the earth, they said to them, "Why do you seek the living among the dead?" (Luke 24:5, NKJV).

The angels' mission was to interpret the empty tomb for the followers of Jesus so they would not misunderstand its significance. The angel's message was intended to prepare the disciples for an actual meeting with the risen Christ. "Go quickly and tell His disciples that He is risen from the dead, and indeed He is going before you into Galilee; there you will see Him. Behold, I have told you" (Matt. 28:7, NKJV; cf. Mark 16:;7; Luke 24:9). Women were

> Angels had the privilege of being the first to announce the resurrection of Jesus Christ.

given the privilege of being the first to tell the stunning news that Jesus who had died on the cross of Calvary was alive!

Angels Were Present At Jesus' Ascension To Heaven (Acts 1:10-11)

Jesus spoke frequently with his apostles following his resurrection. After Christ had given his apostles final instructions, he ascended into heaven. As the disciples stood watching, the angels said, "Men of Galilee, why do you stand gazing up into heaven? This same Jesus, who was taken up from you into heaven, will so come in like manner as you saw Him go into heaven" (Acts 1:11, NKJV). These angels assured the disciples that when the final day comes, Jesus will return "in like manner"—physically and visibly—from heaven to call his children to meet him in the air (1 Thess. 4:16; Rev. 1:7).

Angels Will Accompany Jesus Christ Upon His Return (Matt. 25:31; Mark 8:38; 1 Thess. 4:16; 2 Thess. 1:6-10)

Jesus Christ's appearance to judge the world will be splendid and glorious. When Christ comes in his glory to judge the world, He will bring all His holy angels with Him. This glorious Person will have a glorious entourage, His holy angels, who not only will be His attendants, but ministers of His justice. They shall come with Him both for glory and service.

Jesus Christ came to earth surrounded by myriads of these ministering spirits to assist Him in the execution of his holy work. Jesus also ascended into heaven in a cloud of glory attended by a guard of mighty angels. In like manner, Jesus will return with a host of mighty angels to execute judgment upon the world of mankind.

Questions:

1. Why do you believe God sent angels to minister to Jesus Christ? _____

   _____

   _____

2. Describe the role that the angel Gabriel played in the birth of John the Baptist. _____

   _____

   _____

3. List the prophecies that Gabriel told Mary that her son would fulfill.

   _____

   _____

4. What lesson can we learn from Mary's reaction to Gabriel's announcement of Christ's birth? _____

   _____

   _____

5. Why did the angels have to encourage Joseph to marry Mary? _____

   _____

6. Explain your personal reaction to the announcement of Christ's birth by the angels in Luke 2:18-15. _____

   _____

7. Why do you believe the angels told Joseph to flee to Egypt and take his family? _____

_____

_____

8. Where did God tell Joseph to settle with his young family? Why? _____

_____

_____

9. What was the purpose of Christ being led by the Holy Spirit into temptation? _____

_____

10. Summarize the temptation of Jesus in Matthew 4 and the role that angels played. _____

_____

_____

11. Why did the angels aid Jesus Christ in the Garden of Gethsemane? ____

_____

_____

12. Why was it necessary for an angel to roll away the stone from Christ's tomb? _____

_____

13. Summarize the angels' role in the announcement of Christ's resurrection.

_____

_____

_____

14. What will be the role of angels in Christ's return for judgment? _____

_____

Angel Encounters in the Book of Acts

Jesus Christ ascended to heaven at the beginning of the book of Acts. The Book of Acts reveals the story of the emergence and spread of the early church following Christ's resurrection and ascension. Angels appeared on numerous occasions to support Christ's apostles as they met the challenge of spreading the gospel to the world. Luke recounts what happened first in Jerusalem, then tells about the spread of the gospel from Palestine to nearby regions, and traces the missionary activities of the apostle Paul and his companions as they carried the gospel to the major cities of the Roman Empire. Angels appeared frequently throughout this period. In fact, given that the story of Acts is compressed into a span of thirty years, there are more accounts of angel intervention during this period than in any other period of biblical history, excluding the exodus of the children of Israel from Egypt.

Angels Spoke To The Apostles As They Watched Jesus Ascend Into Heaven (Acts 1:10-11)

Jesus Christ spoke frequently with his apostles following his resurrection from the dead. In Acts chapter one Jesus commanded the apostles that they should not depart from Jerusalem. The city of Jerusalem was the place where Christ had been slain and where the resurrection was first proclaimed. Jerusalem was to be the location where the apostles would receive the gift or power of the Holy Spirit, where the Gospel of Christ would first be preached, and where Christ's kingdom would first be established. The Old Testament prophets had declared that Jerusalem should be the place where the Gospel would first be proclaimed (Isa. 2:2-4; Joel 2:28-32; Dan. 2:44-45).

The apostles of Christ were told to wait in Jerusalem for the promise of the Holy Spirit from God the Father (John 14:16; 15:26; 16:13). The Holy Spirit would guide them into all truth and give them the words needed to complete their work of preaching and publishing the gospel of Christ to all nations. They must wait for the Holy Spirit so that they might speak on the great day of the inauguration of the kingdom of Christ, as the Spirit "gave them utterance" (Acts 2:4). The conditions of citizenship in the kingdom must be revealed by the Spirit of God.

Jesus Christ ascended into heaven in a cloud of glory following his final instructions to his apostles (Acts 1:6-9). While the apostles stood watching Christ's ascension, two angels, in the form of men, appear in white, a color in which angels often appeared, to show their purity, and also to represent the joyfulness of their errand. The angels declared to the apostles that this Jesus whom they beheld ascending up into heaven, would come again to judge the world, and would so come again in like manner, that is, visibly, in a cloud, by

> While the apostles stood watching Christ's ascension, two angels, in the form of men, appear in white, a color in which angels often appeared, to show their purity, and also to represent the joyfulness of their errand.

his own power, with the like majesty as they saw him go into heaven (Acts 1:10-11). These two angels were carrying out their God-given function—they were delivering God's message to the apostles of Jesus Christ. This angelic message was designed to comfort the apostles. Though their Master and Friend was taken from them, yet he was not removed forever. Christ will come again.

An Angel Releases The Apostles From Prison (Acts 5:17-29)

The Holy Spirit was received by the apostles of Christ in Jerusalem on the Day of Pentecost (Acts 2:1-4). Peter and the other apostles preached the first gospel sermon. Three lines of evidence were used to prove that Jesus Christ was the Messiah or promised redeemer of Israel:

1. Jesus proved himself to be the Son of God by miracles, wonders, and signs which he performed among the Israelites (Acts 2:22).
2. Jesus fulfilled all the Old Testament prophecies concerning the Messiah and the outpouring of the Holy Spirit upon the apostles of Christ (Acts 2:25-30).
3. The resurrection of Christ was the final proof of his deity (Acts 2:31-36).

The apostles' preaching on this occasion led to some three thousand conversions to Christianity (Acts 2:37-41).

Many fresh questions arose concerning Jesus following the events on the Day of Pentecost. Could Jesus truly be the promised Messiah after all? Peter and John healed a lame man at the gate of the temple and used the occasion to preach another powerful sermon concerning Jesus Christ (Acts 3). The preaching of the gospel of Christ and the miracles performed by the apostles won the approval of the residents of Jerusalem, and many were converted to Christianity. "Many of those who heard the word believed; and the number of the men came to be about five thousand" (Acts 4:4, NKJV). The early church grew rapidly. The three thousand converts on the Day of Pentecost had grown to five thousand. The opposition to the gospel of Christ by the priests, the Sadducees and the Sanhedrin court also increased rapidly. The leadership of the Israelites was infuriated by the response of the people in Jerusalem to the gospel of Christ (Acts 4:1-2).

The apostles continued to heal the sick and perform miracles and signs among the people (Acts 5:12-13). The converts to the Lord continued to increase. "Believers were increasingly added to the Lord, multitudes of both men and women" (Acts 5:14, NKJV). The Jewish officials began to panic "and laid their hands on the apostles and put them in the common prison" (Acts 5:18, NKJV). During the night an angel of the Lord opened the gates of the prison, escorted the apostles out, and then apparently closed the gates and locked them, while remaining unnoticed by the prison guards (Acts 5:19). The angel commanded the apostles to continue preaching the message of Life. "Go, stand in the temple and speak to the people all the words of this life" (Acts 5:20, NKJV). This angel encounter demonstrated God's protection of his apostles in their mission to spread the gospel throughout the world.

An Angel Sent Philip On A Mission (Acts 8:26-40)

The Jews could not tolerate the doctrine of Christ's resurrection; for this point being proved demonstrated Christ's innocence and their enormous guilt in his crucifixion. As the apostles continued to strongly insist on the resurrection of Christ, the persecution against the early Christians greatly intensified. Stephen was stoned to death for preaching the truth concerning God's plan for the salvation of mankind (Acts 7). The Jewish officials had become so embittered by the zeal and success of the apostles, and by their frequent charges of murder in putting the Son of God to death, that they resolved at once to put an end to the progress and success of the early Christians. The persecution against the church at Jerusalem became so intense that many of the believers were forced to leave the city. These Christians were scattered throughout Judea and into Samaria (Acts 8:1), and "those who were scattered went everywhere preaching the word" (Acts 8:4, NKJV). Wherever the early Christian went they talked about Jesus. The providence of God can easily be seen upon this occasion. This persecution dispersed many of the early Christians and, contrary to the hope and design of its authors, became in the hand of God, the means of spreading the Gospel by sending forth members of the Church into different regions, who taught, preached, and worked miracles. Out of the darkness of persecution the Lord brought forth the light and transmission of the Gospel.

Philip, one of the early evangelists, went to the city of Samaria and preached Christ unto those who resided there (Acts 8:5). The people of Samaria were very receptive to the truth that Philip preached and the miracles he performed. "They believed Philip as he preached the things concerning the kingdom of God and the name of Jesus Christ, both men and women were baptized" (Acts 8:12, NKJV). The simple facts of the kingdom of Christ were set forth before the people of Samaria, and, upon belief of these truths, attended by a willingness to comply with the requirements of the gospel, they were baptized without delay. This was but a faithful execution of the great commission, which says, "He that believeth and is baptized shall be saved" (Mark 16:16).

The preaching and miracles performed by Philip stimulated a great restoration to the Lord in the city of Samaria. During this great success Philip experienced an angel encounter. "Now an angel of the Lord spoke to Philip, saying, 'Arise and go toward the south along the road which goes down from Jerusalem to Gaza.' This is desert" (Acts 8:26, NKJV). The angel did not explain the message but simply told Philip where to go, and Philip obeyed without question (Acts 8:27). Philip's quick response to the angelic message is a tribute to his strong faith; it is also an indication of the self-authenticating nature of the angelic messages. It would seem to make no sense for Philip to leave the success of Samaria and head into a deserted region, but he did not question the directions, he simply followed the angel's instructions.

The purpose of Philip's angel encounter would soon become clear. On the road from Jerusalem to Gaza Philip met the "Ethiopian eunuch" who was a high government official who supervised the Queen of Ethiopia's treasury (Acts 8:27). The eunuch had come to Jerusalem to worship according to the Law of Moses. The Holy Spirit directed Philip to meet the eunuch and teach him the gospel of Jesus Christ. The eunuch was reading about the suffering and death of Jesus Christ from Isaiah 53, but did not understand it. Philip ex-

No one receives a direct calling from God, Christ, the Holy Spirit or an angel to accept the gospel plan of salvation.

plained the passage to him, and revealed to the eunuch the gospel of Christ. The eunuch believed, and he was baptized into Jesus Christ (Acts 8:36-39).

What lessons can we learn from Philip and the Ethiopian Eunuch? First, no one receives a direct calling from God, Christ, the Holy Spirit or an angel to accept the gospel plan of salvation. Those individuals who will be saved by the gospel of Christ must come to a knowledge of the truth in exactly the same manner as the eunuch. "So then faith comes by hearing, and hearing by the word of God" (Rom. 10:17, NKJV). God commands that everyone "hear" the gospel of Christ in order to be saved. "He said to them, 'Go into all the world and preach the gospel to every creature'" (Mark 16:15, NKJV). God's plan for the salvation of the world is through the preaching of the Gospel of Christ. "For since in the wisdom of God the world through its wisdom did not come to know God, God was well-pleased through the foolishness of the message preached to save those who believe" (1 Cor. 1:21, NASB). Second, we see the providence of God in the conversion of the Ethiopian eunuch. Philip was called away from preaching to multitudes in Samaria to teach a single individual, the eunuch. God, through His providence, will provide each sincere and honest individual who is looking for the truth an opportunity to hear and see the truth.

Cornelius Was Directed By Angels To Send For Peter (Acts 10)

Cornelius was a centurion of the Roman army who lived in Caesarea, a city on the Mediterranean coast with a spectacular man-made harbor. Herod the Great had constructed the city of Caesarea in honor of Augustus Caesar and it was the seat of the Roman government in Israel. Cornelius was described as "a devout man, and one who feared God with all his household, and gave many alms to the Jewish people, and prayed to God continually" (Acts 10:2, NASB). Cornelius believed in one God, the Creator of heaven and earth, and had a reverence for His glory and authority, and a dread of offending Him by sin. Cornelius had taught his entire family to have respect for God. Cornelius took care that not himself only, but all his, should serve the Lord. Every good man will do what he can that those about him may be good also. Cornelius was also a very benevolent man; "he gave many alms." Though he was a Gentile, he was willing to contribute to the relief of anyone that was a real object of charity. Cornelius prayed to God always. He was constant in his prayer to God. Wherever the fear of God rules in the heart, it will appear both in works of charity and of piety.

What more did Cornelius, this God-fearing and outstandingly moral man, need to do to be pleasing to God? He needed to hear and obey the gospel of Christ in order to be saved from his sins. An angel appeared to Cornelius and directed him to send to Joppa for Peter, to instruct him in the way of salvation. God had heard the prayers of Cornelius and seen his benevolent acts of kindness. "He said to him, 'Your prayers and alms have ascended as a memorial before God'"(Acts 10:4, NASB). Cornelius, a Gentile who believed in God and who demonstrated his faith by his generosity and his commitment to prayer, was given an opportunity to learn the truth through the Apostle Peter.

When the Apostle Peter arrived he found Cornelius and his family and close friends assembled to "hear all that had been commanded by the Lord" (Acts 10:33, NASB). Peter shared the gospel with Cornelius and his entire

> No one receives a direct calling from God, Christ, the Holy Spirit or an angel to accept the gospel plan of salvation.

> Wherever the fear of God rules in the heart, it will appear both in works of charity and of piety

household. Peter began his sermon with God's most basic principle of salvation. "Then Peter opened his mouth and said: 'In truth I perceive that God shows no partiality. But in every nation whoever fears Him and works righteousness is accepted by Him'" (Acts 10:34-35, NKJV). God does not show favoritism toward a nation, or a group of people, or an individual. God's standard of salvation is the same for everyone. Those who desire salvation must have faith and trust in God that leads them to respect God and be obedient to his will. Cornelius and his household believed the gospel preached by Peter and were "baptized in the name of the Lord" (Acts 10:48, NKJV).

Cornelius and his household were the first Gentiles to become Christians, and this event marked a turning point in the early church. Within a few decades the major congregations of the Lord's church throughout the Roman world would be made up predominantly of Gentile converts. The angel encounter of Cornelius is another example of God providing an honest and good man the opportunity to hear the truth of the gospel. The providence of God provided the preacher for the one who needed to hear the truth. The angel that spoke to Cornelius sent a person to share the gospel message, as was also the case with the Ethiopian Eunuch in Acts 8. The angel did not share the gospel directly with either man. Everyone today must "hear" the good news through the apostles of Christ as recorded in God's written word.

An Angel Releases Peter From Prison (Acts 12:1-19)

King Herod Agrippa laid his hands on some of the members of the Lord's church, and he endeavored to violently oppress the church. Herod desired popularity and was eager to satisfy the Jewish authorities, therefore he sought to ruin the Christians. Herod began by afflicting the members of the Lord's body by imprisoning them, fining them, spoiling their houses and goods, and other ways molesting them; but afterwards he proceeded to greater instances of cruelty. Herod had the apostle James killed with a sword (Acts 12:1-2).

The murder of the apostle James was popular with the Jewish authorities. This is the principle on which Herod acted. It was not from a sense of right; it was not to do justice and protect the innocent; it was not to discharge the appropriate duties of a king; but it was to promote his own popularity.

The apostle Peter was the next object of attack. Peter was one of the most conspicuous men in the church. Peter had made himself particularly obnoxious to the Jewish authorities by his severe and overpowering discourses, and by his success in winning men to Christ. The apostle Peter was seized by Herod, imprisoned, and marked for execution after the Passover feast.

Peter's imprisonment moved the members of the Lord's body to constant prayer (Acts 12:5). The Almighty God heard the petition of the church and commissioned an angel to immediately deliver Peter from prison and from the power of his enemies. The apostle Peter was bound with two chains and under close guard in prison when his angel encounter occurred. "An angel of the Lord stood by him, and a light shone in the prison; and he struck Peter on the side and raised him up, saying, 'Arise quickly!' And his chains fell off his hands. Then the angel said to him, 'Gird yourself and tie on your sandals'; and so he did. And he said to him, 'Put on your garment and follow me'" (Acts 12:7-8, NKJV). The angel led Peter out of the prison, the iron gate

> The angel encounter of Cornelius is another example of God providing an honest and good man the opportunity to hear the truth of the gospel.

> The Almighty God heard the petition of the church and commissioned an angel to immediately deliver Peter from prison and from the power of his enemies.

opening "of its own accord" (Acts 12:10). During these events Peter thought he was having a dream or vision. When the angel departed and Peter found himself in the streets of the city alone, he finally realized that the angel was real. Angels are God's guardians who protect the children of God from harm.

An Angel Punishes Herod For His Pride (Acts 12:20-23)

King Herod has sensed the hostility of the Jewish leadership toward the disciples of Christ. Herod killed the apostle James and imprisoned the apostle Peter. An angel released Peter before Herod could have him killed; but the angel's intervention into the life of Herod did not end with Peter's release.

Herod was proud and arrogant, he loved the praise of men. He was a true enemy of the children of God. Herod was hailed as a god by the people of Tyre and Sidon and he accepted their worship and praise. "Then immediately an angel of the Lord struck him, because he did not give glory to God. And he was eaten by worms and died" (Acts 12:23, NKJV). The angels of the Lord who released Peter from prison also were God's agents of justice who executed God's judgment upon Herod and condemned him to a painful death. Herod, who anticipated the death of Peter, died a sudden and painful death inflicted by the angel of the Lord because he failed to glorify God.

Paul Was Encouraged By An Angel During A Storm At Sea (Acts 27)

The apostle Paul was on a ship heading toward Rome when a storm drove the ship off course and threatened the life of everyone on board. After many days at sea, when all the passengers and crew believed they were going to perish, Paul reported that he had been visited by an angel.

"I urge you to take heart, for there will be no loss of life among you, but only of the ship. For there stood by me this night an angel of the God to whom I belong and whom I serve, saying, 'Do not be afraid, Paul; you must be brought before Caesar; and indeed God has granted you all those who sail with you'" (Acts 27:22-24, NKJV). Paul had a strong faith and confidence in God and his messenger. "Therefore take heart, men, for I believe God that it will be just as it was told me" (Acts 27:25, NKJV).

The apostle Paul identified the angel's message as God's revelation. The angel promised, and Paul believed God. The angelic message was one of encouragement. Paul was encouraged not to lose his faith in God and his divine protection. The God whom Paul loved and trusted would guard and guide those who trust him.

When we compare the stories of angel encounters found in the Old Testament with those in the New Testament, we find striking and compelling similarities. In both Testaments we find:

- Angels guide and direct believers

- Angels are depicted as guardians who protect believers from harm

- Angels deliver God's messages, provide instruction and predict the future

- Angels are sent by God to humans to prepare hearts, to commission them for special service, and to encourage them.

Angels were active in the lives of believers in both the Old Testament and the New Testament periods. Throughout history angels have been God's ministers, sent to serve those who are heirs of salvation (Heb. 1:14).

Questions:

1. What was the purpose of the angels at the ascension of Jesus Christ?

    _____

    _____

2. What message did the angels give to the apostles? _____

    _____

3. Describe the results of the preaching and miracles of the apostles in Jerusalem. _____

    _____

    _____

4. Why were the apostles imprisoned in Acts 5? _____

    _____

5. Why did the angel set the apostles free in Acts 5? _____

    _____

6. What was the commission given to the apostles following their release from prison? _____

    _____

7. Describe the role of the angel in the preaching of Philip to the Ethiopian Eunuch._____

    _____

8. What is the God-given means of receiving knowledge of the Gospel of Christ? _____

    _____

9. Why did the angel tell Cornelius to send for Peter?_____

    _____

10. Why did the angel not tell Cornelius what to do to be saved?_____

    _____

11. Describe the role of the angel in Peter's release from prison. _____

    _____

12. Why was Peter released from the control of Herod? _____

    _____

13. Why was Herod eaten of worms?_____

    _____

14. What encouragement did Paul receive from an angel and why? _____

    _____

15. What lesson can we learn from the angel encounters in the Book of Acts?

    _____

God's Rule in the Nations of the World

> However, God does have the ability to use men, whether good or wicked, to accomplish whatever He desires.

The Bible is a revelation of Almighty God and his concern and relationship with mankind as he works for man's good upon this earth and his glory throughout eternity. Jehovah is revealed in the Bible as the creator of the universe and mankind. "By the word of the LORD the heavens were made, and all the host of them by the breath of His mouth" (Psa. 33:6, NKJV). This universe in which man lives shows design, purpose, and orderliness which proves that it came from the hand of an intelligent creator who possesses a purpose for this world and mankind.

The word "providence" is generally used to describe God's working in the natural and spiritual realms. In reference to God, providence means foresight and forethought which enables the infinite God to create a universe that He could control by His laws and give man the freedom of choice, but God is able to overrule in that universe and still achieve his purpose. God rules in three areas: (1) the physical creation (inanimate-material); (2) the animal creation; and (3) the moral creation (mankind).

God rules in nations. Since the beginning of time, God has exercised control over nations and their kings. God can and does raise up certain men to fulfill his purpose. God does not make man do anything against his own will. Man formulates his own personality and exercises his own will. However, God does have the ability to use men, whether good or wicked, to accomplish whatever He desires. There comes a time in a moral world when a judgment must come. Judgment always comes when there is not enough salt (righteous influence) to save a nation. Our purpose in this lesson is to show God's rule and control of nations in the past and to make application to God's present control of the world.

What Is Providence?

The biblical concept of "providence" carries the idea of God's forethought and foresight in creating a material world where he has the ability to exercise his control and will, while at the same time providing mankind the freedom of choice to exercise his will. The necessary components of God's providence are:

- God is the divine creator of our universe and he has the power to control his creation (Gen. 1:1; Psa. 148:5; Rev. 4:11).

- God continues to oversee and sustain his universe today. He now "upholds all things by the word of his power" (Heb. 1:3).

- God has provided mankind laws to govern and guide his life upon this earth both in the physical and moral worlds. The laws by which man's world operates is an expression of God's will for man.

- Mankind is subject to all laws of nature and will suffer consequences upon violation of natural law. Blessing is the result of obedience; accidents, suffering, and death are the consequence of disobedience.

- The laws of God are designed for the moral and spiritual training of mankind (Jas. 1:2-5; 1 Pet. 1:5-6).

- God has the power and ability to allow mankind the freedom of choice in his daily life, but also to use man's choices to accomplish his purpose.

- God can directly alter the course of human events, if he wills, in answer to the prayers of his children (Jas. 5:13-18; 1 Pet. 3:12).

God is the creator, lawgiver and governor of the universe in which mankind lives. God does not make mistakes; but always performs what is righteous and His purpose is always for man's benefit. God will always operate in harmony with His will and His character. God does not force mankind to obey His will. Mankind has the God-given freedom of choice to do with his life as he desires. Throughout this study we have demonstrated how God has used angels to carry out and accomplish his will. This lesson will illustrate how God in his providence has used angels in the control of nations down through history.

Jehovah Is King Of The Nations

God had a purpose or a plan for the eternal salvation of mankind before the creation of the world (Eph. 1:3-5). The Word of God reveals the fulfillment of God's plan. In order to accomplish His purpose, God created a world that he could control. God chose Abraham and his seed as the nation through whom he would fulfill his eternal plan. God made three promises to Abraham:

1. The Land of Canaan as an inheritance;

2. That Abraham's seed or children would become a great nation;

3. That from the lineage of Abraham, all families of the earth shall be blessed (Gen. 12:1-3).

The Word of God reveals God's providential care for the nation of Israel in order to bring about the fulfillment of his promises. Jehovah has also demonstrated his control of heathen nations down through history, who have attempted to destroy the people of God and to overthrow the worship of Jehovah. God exercises universal control of nations for the working out of his purpose. The apostle Paul stated that, "He [God who made the world] has made from one blood every nation of men to dwell on all the face of the earth, and has determined their preappointed times and the boundaries of their dwellings" (Acts 17:26, NKJV). The psalmist David declared God's universal rule, "For the kingdom is the LORD'S, and He rules over the nations" (Psa. 22:28, NKJV). The prophet Jeremiah affirms that no one can compare to the power and glory of God Almighty. "Inasmuch as there is none like You, O LORD (You are great, and Your name is great in might), Who would not fear You, O King of the nations? For this is Your rightful due.

For among all the wise men of the nations, And in all their kingdoms, there is none like You" (Jer. 10:6-7, NKJV). In this lesson we will examine God's use of nations to accomplish his plan and purpose. God has used his angels to exact judgment upon both individuals and nations who failed to be obedient to his will.

The People Of Noah's Day (Gen. 6-9)

Mankind was created by God as moral creatures possessing the ability to choose one's own actions. God has always provided laws in the physical and spiritual world to control and direct mankind for man's benefit. The spiritual laws are given by God to govern the free moral agency of mankind. Obedience or disobedience to God's law always brings consequences that produce good or evil results. The history of mankind details the fact that God will always bring judgment upon a nation or an individual in consequence of their violation and rejection of divine law and their rebellion against God. God in his providence allows a people or a nation to exist until their spiritual and moral righteousness has disappeared.

In the days following Adam and Eve's expulsion from the Garden of Eden the whole earth became corrupt and God decided to destroy it. "The LORD saw that the wickedness of man was great in the earth, and that every intent of the thoughts of his heart was only evil continually. And the LORD was sorry that He had made man on the earth, and He was grieved in His heart. So the LORD said, 'I will destroy man whom I have created from the face of the earth, both man and beast, creeping thing and birds of the air, for I am sorry that I have made them'" (Gen. 6:5-7, NKJV). One man found favor in the sight of Jehovah because of his righteousness, that man was Noah. "Noah found grace in the eyes of the LORD. This is the genealogy of Noah. Noah was a just man, perfect in his generations. Noah walked with God" (Gen. 6:8-9, NKJV). God in his grace extended the period before the destruction of the world for one hundred twenty years to allow the world to repent and return to God. Noah spent the one hundred twenty years preparing the ark in the sight of all and preaching righteousness to the people. The people of Noah's day refused to see and heed the warnings, and only eight persons were prepared to enter the ark before the flood and destruction swept them away. God is patient and allows time for people and nations to repent, but God's longsuffering will always end in destruction for the disobedient. "[God] did not spare the ancient world, but saved Noah, one of eight people, a preacher of righteousness, bringing in the flood on the world of the ungodly" (2 Pet. 2:5, NKJV; cf. 1 Pet. 3:20). There is no mention of angelic activity during the period of Noah.

The Children of Israel

God in his providence chose Abraham and the nation of Israel as the ones through whom Jesus Christ would come into the world; and he controlled the direction of the nation of Israel to achieve his purpose. In order to fulfill the promises to Abraham, God had to control the destiny of both the children of Abraham and the nations which surrounded them. God has the ability to use the choices and decisions that both individuals and nations make to accomplish his purpose, without interfering in man's free choice.

Abraham had two sons, Ishmael and Isaac. God chose Isaac as the one

> The history of mankind details the fact that God will always bring judgment upon a nation or an individual in consequence of their violation and rejection of divine law and their rebellion against God.

through whom the promises would be fulfilled. Isaac had two sons, Esau and Jacob. God selected Jacob as the promised seed. Jacob was blessed with twelve sons and in the providence of God, Joseph was chosen as the one who would help the sons of Jacob survive a severe famine and grow into a great nation in the land of Egypt. Angels played an active role in the call to God's service and protection of Abraham, Isaac, and Jacob.

The story of Joseph and the events that brought Jacob's family into the land of Egypt is one of the best illustrations of the providence of God. The story of Joseph and his brothers reveals the beginning of the Israelite nation. God does not always need to work a miracle to accomplish his purpose. God used the normal events in the daily life of Joseph to fulfill his purpose with the exception being the dreams of Joseph and others and their interpretation. Each incident in Joseph's life played an important role in the moving of Jacob and his family into Egypt and their development into a great nation (Gen. 45:5-8; 50:19-20). Nothing that happened in the life of Joseph was without significance. God was able to take a Hebrew shepherd boy and transform him into the most powerful individual upon this earth.

The People of Egypt (Psalms 78:43-51)

It has been pointed out that God had a purpose or plan for man's redemption before the foundation of the world (Eph. 1:3-14). God in his providence selected the Israelite nation and directed them to be the people through whom Jesus Christ would come to redeem the world from sin. A terrible famine struck the Middle East, and only Egypt had a supply of food to ensure the nation of Israel's survival. Abraham's grandson, Jacob, led his small family into Egypt to escape the famine. The majority of the time that the descendants of Abraham were in Egypt they were in the bondage of slavery to Pharaoh and the Egyptians (Exod. 1:7-14). During the time of the bondage they became a great nation of people.

God raised up his servant Moses to deliver the Israelites from Egyptian bondage. God demonstrated his power and might through the ten plagues brought upon Pharaoh and the land of Egypt (Exod. 7-12). God proved to the world that he was the only true and living God.

The Children of Israel were rescued by unmistakable acts of divine power, and the Egyptians were punished for decades of cruel oppression of God's people. The writer of Psalms details the wonders Jehovah performed "when he worked his signs in Egypt" (Psa. 78:43-51). Psalms 78:49 tells us that God "cast on them the fierceness of His anger, wrath, indignation, and trouble, by sending angels of destruction among them." It appears that God used angels to punish Egypt for their cruelty. Exodus chapter 12 suggests that angels were directly involved in the final plague upon Egypt, in which the firstborn son in every Egyptian household was killed in a single night.

The Inhabitants Of The Land Of Canaan

God's promise to Abraham that his descendants would inherit the land of Canaan was not immediately fulfilled. It would to be over four hundred years before God would give the land of Canaan to Abraham's descendants (Gen. 15:16). The wickedness of these nations of the land of Canaan would cause God to cast them out. "Do not think in your heart, after the LORD your

> The story of Joseph and the events that brought Jacob's family into the land of Egypt is one of the best illustrations of the providence of God.

God has cast them out before you, saying, 'Because of my righteousness the LORD has brought me in to possess this land'; but it is because of the wickedness of these nations that the LORD is driving them out from before you" (Deut. 9:4, NKJV). When a nation fails to serve God they will be destroyed. "The wicked will return to Sheol, Even all the nations who forget God" (Psa. 9:17, NASB). "Righteousness exalts a nation, But sin is a disgrace to any people" (Prov. 14:34, NASB). No nation will go unpunished when its wickedness becomes great in the sight of God (Amos 1-2.

Two passages from the Book of Exodus clearly indicate that angels fought alongside Israel. "For My Angel will go before you and bring you in to the Amorites and the Hittites and the Perizzites and the Canaanites and the Hivites and the Jebusites; and I will cut them off" (Exod. 23:23). "I will send My Angel before you, and I will drive out the Canaanite and the Amorite and the Hittite and the Perizzite and the Hivite and the Jebusite" (Exod. 33:2, NKJV). Angels went before God's people and assisted them in the removal and destruction of a culture whose sinful practices God hated.

The Children of Israel

At the end of the nation of Israel's sojourn in the land of Egypt, God provided safe passage for the Israelites through the Red Sea and into the wilderness of Mount Sinai. The Children of Israel came to Mount Sinai to make an agreement with God Almighty to become his holy nation and chosen people (Exod. 19:3-8). God promised the children of Israel that as long as they were faithful to Him they would prosper in the land, but when they forsook God it would be taken away (Deut. 28; Lev. 26)

The Israelites were bitter, angry and hostile toward God, despite the fact that God had demonstrated his love and care for them by daily providing a special food from heaven. Jehovah would provide for their every need during their wilderness wanderings (Neh. 9:20-21). Following the events at Mount Sinai, the children of Israel would wander in the wilderness for forty years.

Jehovah disciplined the nation of Israel in the wilderness of Sinai to develop faith and trust in Jehovah and his power alone. When the children of Israel had learned the lessons God had prepared, he drove out the Canaanites and gave their land to his people Israel. The children of Israel were a great nation and they did receive the land of Canaan as an inheritance. God was fulfilling his plan and promise to Abraham.

Throughout the three hundred years that followed the possession of the land of Canaan, the nation of Israel was plagued by repeated apostasies from God and God sending oppression from foreign nations because of the Israelites unfaithfulness. When the oppression became great the Israelites would repent and call upon God for help. God would exalt a deliverer through whom God would free the people. As the period of the judges (deliverers) began to draw to a close the children of Israel cried for a king like the nations around them. God allowed Saul of the tribe of Benjamin to be selected as their first king. Saul failed as a king because of his disobedience to God's will. David, a man after God's own heart, of the tribe of Judah is selected by God to be the family through which Jesus Christ would come into the world.

> When a nation fails to serve God they will be destroyed. "The wicked will return to Sheol, Even all the nations who forget God" (Psa. 9:17, NASB).

Angels and Other Created Spiritual Beings

David's successors would control the throne of God until the Babylonian captivity (586 B.C.)

Following the death of Solomon, the son of David, the nation of Israel was divided into the northern and southern kingdoms, known as Israel and Judah. The northern kingdom of Israel descended deeper into idolatry and moral wickedness, and God declared his intention to bring the nation to an end. "Behold, the eyes of the Lord GOD are on the sinful kingdom, And I will destroy it from the face of the earth; Yet I will not utterly destroy the house of Jacob," Says the LORD" (Amos 9:8, NKJV). "The LORD said to him: "Call his name Jezreel, For in a little while I will avenge the bloodshed of Jezreel on the house of Jehu, And bring an end to the kingdom of the house of Israel" (Hos. 1:4 NKJV). The nation of Israel had become worse than the heathen nations, for they had the word of God and the worship of God which they rejected for idolatry. God used the heathen nation of Assyria to destroy Israel and carry the people into captivity in 721 B.C. "Woe to Assyria, the rod of My anger And the staff in whose hand is My indignation. I will send him against an ungodly nation, And against the people of My wrath I will give him charge, To seize the spoil, to take the prey, And to tread them down like the mire of the streets. Yet he does not mean so, Nor does his heart think so; But it is in his heart to destroy, And cut off not a few nations" (Isa. 10:5-7, NKJV). The kings of Assyria had no intention of doing God's will, but God knew their hearts and used them as a rod of his judgment against Israel.

The Nation of Assyria

The nation of Assyria was used as a tool of God's wrath against sinful nations. The Assyrian army, under the command of Sennacherib, invaded the land of Canaan and crushed all the fortified cities and easily captured the northern Kingdom of Israel. Sennacherib and the Assyrian army then surrounded the city of Jerusalem and expected to easily take the city. When the Assyrian officer demanded the surrender of a defenseless Jerusalem and ridiculed the God of Israel, King Hezekiah of Judah prayed for divine intervention, and the Lord responded (2 Kings 19:3-7). The Lord sent an angel who killed 185,000 Assyrian soldiers of all ranks. Sennacherib was forced to return home, and Jerusalem and the people of God were saved (2 Kings 19:35 37). God did not overlook the crimes of Assyria and that nation was also punished for their sinful conduct. "Therefore it shall come to pass, when the Lord has performed all His work on Mount Zion and on Jerusalem, that He will say, 'I will punish the fruit of the arrogant heart of the king of Assyria, and the glory of his haughty looks'" (Isa. 10:12, NKJV; cf: Isa. 10:24-25).

The Nation of Babylon

The nation of Judah was not taken by the Assyrians but would continue until after the Assyrians were overthrown by the Babylonians. The capital city of Assyria, Nineveh was besieged and captured by Nabopolassar, the king of Babylon in 612 B.C. God's divine mercy to the world is seen in the overthrow of wicked nations and God's judgment in world affairs. God's providence exalts men to high places to accomplish his purpose.

By the time that the nation of Babylon was becoming a world power, the

> **God's divine mercy to the world is seen in the overthrow of wicked nations and God's judgment in world affairs. God's providence exalts men to high places to accomplish his purpose.**

nation of Judah had become corrupt and wicked in the sight of God. Jehovah raised up the nation of Babylon as the instrument of his wrath with which to punish the nation of Judah. "Look among the nations and watch - Be utterly astounded! For I will work a work in your days Which you would not believe, though it were told you. For indeed I am raising up the Chaldeans, A bitter and hasty nation Which marches through the breadth of the earth, To possess dwelling places that are not theirs" (Hab. 1:5-6, NKJV). Nebuchadnezzar and the Babylonians would destroy the nation of Judah, which terminated the reign of the Davidic kings over Israel. The nation of Israel was brought to an end as a political kingdom, but they would never be destroyed as a people, remaining a distinct race throughout time (Jer. 30:11; 46:28).

There were three deportations of the people of Judah to Babylon under Nebuchadnezzar: 605, 597, and 586 B.C (Isa. 39:6-7). Daniel was among those Israelites who were part of the first deportation (Dan. 1:1-6). The book of Daniel is a picture of God's people during the Babylonian Captivity. Daniel sought to encourage the people of God in a foreign land by assuring them of their return to Jerusalem and the land of Canaan and of the future glory of the spiritual kingdom of God. The purpose of the book of Daniel is, (1) To prove that God will protect his people in a heathen nation; (2) God will establish his spiritual kingdom and carry it out to its ultimate destiny; and (3) To prove the fact that God rules in the political kingdoms of men.

God sets up over the kingdoms of men whomsoever He wills (Dan. 2: 36-37; 4:17-25; 32; 5:17-23).

The Medio-Persian Empire

Jehovah exalted the Medes and Persians as his instrument of judgment against Babylon (Isa. 13:17; Jer. 51:11). The Medes and the Persians destroyed the city of Babylon in 539 B.C. God also prophesied that Cyrus the King of Persia would permit the children of Israel to return to Jerusalem and rebuild the temple of God (Isa. 44:28-45:7). Cyrus is described as the "anointed" of God. God says of Cyrus, "I have named you, though you have not known Me. I am the LORD, and there is no other; There is no God besides Me. I will gird you, though you have not known Me" (Isa. 45:4-5, NKJV). Cyrus was being used by God to carry out God's purpose, even though he did not realize he was an instrument of God.

Fifty-eight years after the return of the Israelites to their homeland of Canaan, an incident occurred in the Medio-Persian Empire that threatened extinction of the Hebrew people. This extinction of God's people was prevented by one of God's outstanding acts of providence. Esther, a Jewish orphan girl, is exalted to be the queen of Ahasuerus, the monarch of the Persian Empire ca. 486-465 B.C. Esther was able to use her influence with the King to save the Hebrew people from certain destruction (Esth. 4:13-17).

The Empires of Greece and Rome

The last two world empires to be mentioned in the book of Daniel are Alexander the Great and the Greco-Macedonian Empire and the Roman Empire (Dan. 8). The spiritual kingdom of God was to be established during the days of the Roman Empire (Dan. 2:44-45). God is in control of his entire universe, which includes the kingdoms and governments of men. This should give

> God is in control of his entire universe, which includes the kingdoms and governments of men. This should give every Christian confidence and hope that everything will work for our good as children of God.

Angels and Other Created Spiritual Beings

every Christian confidence and hope that everything will work for our good as children of God.

What About God's Rule In Nations Today?

God is still in control of the civil governments of this world (Rom. 13: 1-7). The destruction of war is God's righteous judgment against wicked people who are not fit to survive and continue. The United States will survive as long as there are enough good moral people to be a positive influence for good

God chose Abraham whose descendants would become a great nation through which God could develop His purpose of providing the world a Savior, Jesus Christ. Despite the constant rebellion of the children of Israel in turning to idolatry and the efforts of heathen nations to destroy the people of God, God's plan and purpose for mankind has been fulfilled. God's providence preserved a faithful remnant through which the redeemer came into the world.

God's providence is shown throughout the centuries of glory and shame, of faithfulness and unfaithfulness, of God's use of individuals and nations to accomplish his eternal purpose. Even so, man's freedom of will and power of choice were never overruled or violated by Jehovah.

Questions

1. Define "providence." _____

   _____

   _____

2. List the necessary components of God's providence: _____

   _____

   _____

3. Describe God's eternal plan for the salvation of mankind. _____

   _____

   _____

4. Why does God have control of the nations of the world? _____

   _____

   _____

5. Why did God destroy the world by water during Noah's time?_____

   _____

6. How does the story of Joseph demonstrate God's providential care of his people? _____

   _____

   _____

7. Describe God's purpose in bringing the destruction upon Egypt. _____

   _____

   _____

8. Why did God allow the children of Israel to destroy the nations in the land of Canaan? _____

   _____

9. What conditions were required of the children of Israel to retain the land of Canaan? _____

_____

10. Describe how God used the nation of Assyria to accomplish his purpose.

_____

_____

_____

11. Why did God allow his people to be carried into Babylonian captivity?

_____

_____

_____

12. Who was the instrument used of God to return his people to Israel?

_____

_____

_____

13. Summarize how the story of Esther is an example of the providence of God. _____

_____

_____

14. Who rules in the kingdoms of men today?_____

_____

_____

The Providence of God and The Individual

God in His providence controls His inanimate and animate world. God in His foresight and forethought created the world in such a way that He could bring His divine and eternal purpose to its desired completion, without arbitrarily forcing His will upon the will of man. God so created man that He could use man's goodness or wickedness to accomplish His purpose. Before the foundation of the world, God designed a plan for man's redemption from sin. God exercised such foresight in the whole creation that He could and would bring His plan to its ultimate and complete consummation and perfection. God's presence and control of all things gives the child of God assurance and confident optimism in this physical world. Our purpose in this lesson is to ask the question, *"What does God do for the Christian today?"*

Jesus Christ Rules In National And Spiritual Kingdoms

When the New Testament opens, the Roman Empire rules the world and the time had come for God to set up His kingdom which would never be destroyed, as foretold in the book of Daniel. "And in the days of these kings the God of heaven will set up a kingdom which shall never be destroyed; and the kingdom shall not be left to other people; it shall break in pieces and consume all these kingdoms, and it shall stand forever" (Dan. 2:44, NKJV). John the Baptist was sent by God to prepare the way for the Lord, heralding the arrival of the Christ and the approach of the kingdom of Old Testament hope. Jesus Christ came to fulfill God's eternal purpose. "Jesus came to Galilee, preaching the gospel of the kingdom of God, and saying, 'The time is fulfilled, and the kingdom of God is at hand. Repent, and believe in the gospel'" (Mark 1:14-15, NKJV). Jesus Christ came to the earth when God was ready for him to arrive. "When the fullness of the time had come, God sent forth His Son, born of a woman, born under the law, to redeem those who were under the law, that we might receive the adoption as sons" (Gal. 4:4-5, NKJV).

Jesus Christ as the Son of God, was given all authority in heaven and in earth following His resurrection from the dead. Jesus came and spoke to them, saying, "All authority has been given to Me in heaven and on earth" (Matt. 28:18, NKJV). Jesus Christ was given by God total control over the physical and spiritual forces of this world. "Which He worked in Christ when He raised Him from the dead and seated Him at His right hand in the heavenly places, far above all principality and power and might and dominion, and every name that is named, not only in this age but also in that which is to come. And He put all things under His feet, and gave Him to be head over all things to the church" (Eph. 1:20-22, NKJV). Jesus Christ was advanced above all, and He was set in authority over all, they being made subject to Him. God invested Him with uncontestable authority over all demons, all

> **God's presence and control of all things gives the child of God assurance and confident optimism in this physical world.**

angels in heaven, and all the princes and potentates on earth. All the glory of the upper world, and all the powers of both worlds, is entirely devoted to Him. The Father put all things under His feet. All creation whatsoever is in subjection to Christ; they must either yield Him sincere obedience or fall under the weight of His judgment, and receive their doom from Him. "Who [Christ] has gone into heaven and is at the right hand of God, angels and authorities and powers having been made subject to Him" (1 Pet. 3:22, NKJV). God gave Christ all power both in heaven and in earth. The Father loves the Son, and hath given ALL things into his hands. But that which completes the comfort for the child of God is that Christ is the head over all things to the church; He is entrusted with all power, that is, that He may control of all the affairs of the church for the benefit of God's children. All things in heaven and earth are controlled for God's purpose and man's benefit. The child of God should have great confidence in his life upon this earth and his eternal destiny because God our Father and Jesus Christ have control of our universe and all its affairs.

Jesus Christ rules in the political kingdoms of men. "Jesus Christ, the faithful witness, the firstborn from the dead, and the ruler over the kings of the earth" (Rev. 1:5, NKJV). The Book of Revelation portrays Christ as the One who "was to rule all nations with a rod of iron" (Rev. 12:5, NKJV). The "rod of iron" is symbolic of the fact that Jesus Christ controls the destiny of all nations upon this earth. Christ also rules in his spiritual kingdom or the church. "He [God] put all things under His feet, and gave Him to be head over all things to the church, which is His body, the fullness of Him who fills all in all" (Eph. 1:22-23, NKJV). Jesus Christ is the "head" or authority in His body, the church. The church is the fullness of Christ and enjoys all the spiritual blessings that Christ provides for His people.

The Providence Of God And The Individual

The Hand of God is at work in the earthly life of mankind. The Book of Ecclesiastes is a search for man's purpose upon this earth. The writer of the Book of Ecclesiastes says that he was searching to "see what was good for the sons of men to do under heaven all the days of their lives" (Eccl. 2:3, NKJV). In chapter three of the Book of Ecclesiastes the writer says, "To everything there is a season, a time for every purpose under heaven" (Eccl. 3:1, NKJV). The writer of Ecclesiastes gives fourteen couplets which detail twenty-eight things which have their time and seasons according to the divine will of God (Eccl. 3:2-8). God by His providence governs the world, and has determined particular things and operations to particular times. God has given to man TIME; the space in which all the operations of nature, of animals, and intellectual beings, are carried on; but while nature is steady in its course, and animals faithful to their instincts, man devotes his time to a great variety of purposes; but very frequently to that for which God never intended for man to perform. Sin is a transgression of God's will for mankind or God's purpose. Man is unable to predetermine or control the seasons or their consequences. God gives and God controls. In order to find the true riches and happiness of this earthly life, man must recognize and acknowledge the limitations of his ability and he must be satisfied to enjoy that which God gives him. "Nothing is better for a man than that he should eat and drink, and that his soul should enjoy good in his labor. This also, I saw, was from the hand of God. For who can eat, or who can have enjoyment, more than I? For God gives wisdom and knowledge and joy to a man who is good in His sight; but to the sinner He gives the work of gathering and collecting, that he may give to him who is good before God" (Eccl. 2:24-26 NKJV). God provides by his providence every blessing that man enjoys in his human life. Each one should enjoy his life to the fullest, and be thankful to God.

God promised providential care for those who are His children. "For I considered all this in my heart, so that I could declare it all: that the righteous and the wise and their works are in the hand of God" (Eccl. 9:1, NKJV). Jehovah has since the beginning of time, promised His faithful children His loving care and protection as their Father. "Have you not known? Have you not heard? The everlasting God, the LORD, The Creator of the ends of the earth, Neither faints nor is weary. His understanding is unsearchable. He gives power to the weak, And to those who have no might He increases strength. Even the youths shall faint and be weary, And the young men shall utterly fall, But those who wait on the LORD Shall renew their strength; They shall mount up with wings like eagles, They shall run and not be weary, They shall walk and not faint" (Isa. 40:28-31, NKJV). God has power to bring about salvation, and that power is never exhausted: "He faints not, nor is weary"; he upholds the whole creation, and governs all the creatures, and is neither tired nor toiled; and therefore, no doubt, he has power to relieve his faithful children, whenever they are brought low through suffering. This physical world is full of trials, problems, and disappointments, but with God's help the child of God will always overcome. The child of God who through his faith in God commits himself to God for guidance and protection in this life will find that God will never fail him (Psa. 46:1; 121:1-2; Prov. 3:5-6).

There are no passages in the New Testament that give greater emphasis to the providence of God than Matthew 6:24-34 and Matthew 7:7-11. Jesus focuses attention on God as our Father and His concern for His own and His ability to act on their behalf. The child of God does not have to worry or be concerned about the physical needs of this life because the individual who seeks first God's kingdom and his righteousness, the Savior promises, "all these things shall be added unto you" (Matt. 6:33).

God as a loving Father also provides for the all spiritual needs of His children. The Apostle Paul declared that God has the ability to make all things work for good for His children. "We know that all things work together for good to those who love God, to those who are the called according to His purpose" (Rom. 8:28, NKJV). Nothing can separate the child of God from the love of God except the Christian himself (Rom. 8:31-39: Heb. 13:5-6).

The Christian has the privilege of prayer to a loving Father, when the burdens of this life become too heavy to bear (Jas. 5:13-16; 1 Pet. 5:7). James, who deals with suffering, sickness, and sin says that prayer to God is a solution to the problems of this life. The Apostle Peter says, "The eyes of the LORD are on the righteous, And His ears are open to their prayers; But the face of the LORD is against those who do evil" (1 Pet. 3:12, NKJV). God is not limited in His power and willingness to aid and assist His children.

> **God provides by his providence every blessing that man enjoys in his human life. Each one should enjoy his life to the fullest, and be thankful to God.**

> **God has power to bring about salvation, and that power is never exhausted.**

"Now to Him [God, the Father] who is able to do exceedingly abundantly above all that we ask or think, according to the power that works in us" (Eph. 3:20, NKJV).

The Secret To Happiness

Men crave happiness and pursue it with all their power, but most are not finding it. Happiness is a state of mind, which the environment cannot seriously affect. The condition of happiness is within us. Happiness cannot be purchased with money or by the heaping up of material possessions.

God gave mankind His formula for happiness in this life and the life to come. "Rejoice in the Lord always. Again I will say, rejoice! Let your gentleness be known to all men. The Lord is at hand. Be anxious for nothing, but in everything by prayer and supplication, with thanksgiving, let your requests be made known to God; and the peace of God, which surpasses all understanding, will guard your hearts and minds through Christ Jesus" (Philippians 4:4-7).

1. Be Positive in All Areas of Life: "Rejoice in the Lord always." We should be positive in our outlook on life. We need to look for the good in everyone and every situation. Count your blessings. "Blessed be the Lord, who daily loadeth us with benefits" (Psa. 68:19). Counting blessings instead of supposed misfortunes enables us to see how God has so richly blessed us. We must emphasize the positive and not the negative in our lives. Count your benefits instead of your reverses and it will surprise you how your efficiency and personality will improve.

2. Show Kindness To All Men: "Let your gentleness be known unto all men." If we want true happiness in this life we must be ready to do good unto all men. We have only one life to live upon this earth. We must do as much good as we can in the time we have upon this earth. If we make it to heaven, we must take someone else with us.

3. Live One Day At A Time: "The Lord is at hand." We should live everyday to the fullest. We should live every day as though it were our last day on earth. We have no guarantee of life expectancy upon this earth. Jesus Christ could return at any moment and life and the world as we know it would end. Our personal life could also end without warning. People die tragic and unexpected deaths everyday. One of God's secrets to happiness is to live each day of our life to the fullest.

4. Don't' Worry—Pray: "Be anxious for nothing; but in everything by prayer . . . let your request be made known unto God." Worry is a thought process, and to a great extent is just a habit that we learn. If we trust in God there is no need to worry about the past, present or future. The cure for worry is prayer. The faithful child of God has the privilege of prayer to an omniscient Father who is sensitive to our every need.

The Result is Peace. "The peace of God . . . shall keep your hearts." Peace is the heart's calm faith in God. It is the firm conviction that God will take care of His own. A Christian can learn to rejoice even when without all is dark and dreary. He rejoices in the Lord. Those who will faithfully follow God's will and His formula for happiness are promised peace of mind or true

> Happiness cannot be purchased with money or by the heaping up of material possessions.

happiness. A person who is in a right relationship with God has nothing to fear from God now or in eternity. The person who is right with God also has nothing to fear from man, because God as his loving Father will see that all his needs are provided. This is a peace that the world cannot understand. It can only come to those who love God and follow his will. Do you have this kind of peace and contentment in your life?

Divine providence is a distinctive feature or attribute whereby the omniscience and omnipotence of the infinite God is expressed toward his creation, with special consideration for those of the creation who are faithful and obedient children. Let us believe in God's providence and walk by faith in it. There is no indication of how God uses angels in the lives of Christians today. We know there are no miraculous appearances of angels today.

Questions

1. Explain the prophecy of Daniel 2:44-45. _____
   _____
   _____

2. When did Jesus Christ come to earth to fulfill God's plan? _____
   _____

3. What authority does Christ possess and how did he receive it?_____
   _____
   _____

4. Explain the significance of Christ being the "head of his body, the church." _____
   _____
   _____

5. Summarize how Christ rules in the political kingdoms of men today.
   _____
   _____
   _____

6. How does God control this earth and still give man the freedom of choice? _____
   _____
   _____

7. Explain your understanding of Ecclesiastes 3:1-15. _____
   _____
   _____

8. Summarize the meaning of Isaiah 40:31._____
   _____
   _____

9. List the promises given in Matthew 6:24-34 and Matthew 7:7-11. _____
   _____
   _____

> Divine providence is a distinctive feature or attribute whereby the omniscience and omnipotence of the infinite God is expressed toward his creation, with special consideration for those of the creation who are faithful and obedient children.

10. Explain the meaning of Romans 8:28-39. _____

_____

_____

11. What solution does the Christian have to the cares and sufferings of this life? _____

_____

_____

12. Summarize God's formula for happiness (Phil. 4:4-7). _____

_____

_____